D1122566

Inside Academia

Inside Academia

~

Professors, Politics, and Policies

STEVEN M. CAHN

Rutgers University Press

New Brunswick, Camden, and Newark, New Jersey, and London

Library of Congress Cataloging-in-Publication Data

Names: Cahn, Steven M., author.
Title: Inside academia : professors, politics, and policies / Steven M. Cahn.
Description: New Brunswick, New Jersey : Rutgers University Press, [2018] |
    Includes bibliographical references and index.
Identifiers: LCCN 2018008402| ISBN 9781978801516 (cloth : alk. paper) |
    ISBN 9781978801509 (pbk. : alk. paper) | ISBN 9781978801523 (epub) |
    ISBN 9781978801547 (Web PDF)
Subjects: LCSH: Universities and colleges—United States—Administration. |
    Education, Higher—Aims and objectives—United States. | Education,
    Higher—Curricula—United States. | College teachers—Tenure—
    United States. | College teaching—United States.
Classification: LCC LC2341 .C34 2018 | DDC 378.1/01—dc23
LC record available at https://lccn.loc.gov/2018008402

A British Cataloging-in-Publication record for this book is available
from the British Library.

∞ The paper used in this publication meets the requirements of the
American National Standard for Information Sciences—Permanence of
Paper for Printed Library Materials, ANSI Z39.48-1992.

www.rutgersuniversitypress.org

Manufactured in the United States of America

To my wife,
Marilyn Ross, M.D.

Contents

Preface   ix

1. How Professors View Academia   1
2. Graduate School   5
3. Turning Point   11
4. How Teachers Succeed   16
5. Teaching Graduate Students to Teach   29
6. Changing Departmental Culture   33
7. The Administration   38
8. Choosing Administrators   42
9. Curricular Structure   46
10. The Case for Liberal Education   50
11. Requirements   55
12. Distribution Requirements   59
13. A Core Curriculum   64
14. Departments   73
15. Appointments   76

16. Tenure and Academic Freedom   81

17. A Tenure Case   85

18. Autonomy   90

    Notes   95

    Index   99

Preface

The focus of this book is life in academia. My chief concern is how professors, and secondarily administrators, too often act in ways that do not serve the best interests of their schools or students.

To begin, I present some personal history, a record of those who have most strongly influenced my outlook on the academic world. I first met people who were called "professor" when I entered Columbia College in 1959. I was taught by some of the best, including Montaigne scholar Donald Frame; translator of Spanish and Portuguese Gregory Rabassa; charismatic American historian James P. Shenton; intellectual historian Bernard W. Wishy; world-class philosopher Ernest Nagel, who encouraged me to pursue the study of philosophy; leading musicologist William J. Mitchell; and Richard Franko Goldman, conductor of the Goldman Band. I continued in graduate school at Columbia, where good luck resulted in my overlapping with the time of prominent metaphysician Richard Taylor, whose impact on my career was immense and about whom I write more later. I also had the pleasure of studying with the elegant and eloquent Charles Frankel, who subsequently became U.S. assistant secretary of state for educational and cultural affairs, then president and director of the National Humanities Center. He will always remain for me the ideal combination of teacher, writer, and social activist.

I began my teaching career at Dartmouth College, then all male, where for a semester I led discussion sections of Introductory Philosophy that supported large lectures for all students in the course. There I heard compelling presentations by colleagues Willis Doney, Timothy Duggan, and Bernard Gert.

My first regular position was at Vassar College, then all female. I served with John O'Connor, razor-sharp analyst yet remarkably amiable, who later became executive director of the American Philosophical Association; Frank Tillman, with whom I edited my first anthology, *Philosophy of Art and Aesthetics: From Plato to Wittgenstein*; and Garrett L. Vander Veer, a paragon of academic integrity.

I then moved to New York University, where I felt honored to have an office next to the eminent political philosopher Sidney Hook, whose intellect and courage I greatly admired. Almost every day, I ate lunch with my colleague James Rachels, an up-and-coming ethical theorist. I also chaired the school's Educational Policy Committee, allowing me to work with outstanding scholar-teachers from numerous fields.

I next accepted an offer to head the philosophy department at the University of Vermont, where the previously combined Philosophy and Religion Department had fallen on hard times. During my first year I led a search process in which, after considering more than seven hundred applicants, I recommended the appointment of four: philosopher of science Philip Kitcher, Kant scholar Patricia Kitcher, philosopher of religion William E. Mann, and social philosopher George Sher. All were so early in their academic careers that they had but one publication among them, but eventually each went on to hold a chair in philosophy. Together we turned our department into one of the country's premier undergraduate programs, which it remains to this day.

I then changed direction and spent five years in the foundation world. I worked at the Exxon Education Foundation, where I served as an academic adviser with Leon Bramson, the noted social scientist who had founded the Department of Sociology and Anthropology at Swarthmore College, and with whom I developed an abiding friendship. Then I became the acting head of humanities at the Rockefeller Foundation, where my colleagues were the internationally known historian of philanthropy Kathleen McCarthy and Stephen D. Lavine, formerly an assistant professor of English at the University of Michigan, who would soon become the longtime president of the California Institute of the Arts. I subsequently moved to Washington, D.C., to become the first director of the division of general programs at the National Endowment for the Humanities. There I learned much from my deputy George F. Farr Jr., a onetime member of the English Department at Vassar College and a wizard in developing government projects that benefited our society. Later I became close friends with him and his wife, Judith Farr, the renowned Emily Dickinson scholar who was professor of English at Georgetown University.

I then returned to academia to become a professor of philosophy and administrator at the Graduate Center of the City University of New York, where I served first as dean, then as provost, and finally as acting president. I was fortunate to have as my associate provost Geoffrey Marshall, a scholar of seventeenth-century English literature and Restoration drama, who had been deputy chairman of the National Endowment for the Humanities and brought his remarkable administrative skills to my aid. At the Graduate Center I met many notable scholars but only have space to mention a few: dean of research and biologist Solomon Goldstein, one of the few people I have known who was equally comfortable discussing issues in science, social science, and humanities; celebrated musicologist and distinguished professor Barry Brook; influential philosopher of mind David Rosenthal; Mary Ann Caws, distinguished professor of English, French, and comparative literature, who served as president of both the Modern Language Association and the American Comparative Language Association; and Lillian Feder, distinguished professor of English, classics, and comparative literature, with whom I occasionally conducted a noncredit interdisciplinary colloquium in classics of world literature, open to dissertation-level students from throughout the graduate school.

In the midst of such happy recollections, I confess that I have also met too many professors and administrators whose performance was subpar. They remind me that the academic world harbors its share of ne'er-do-wells.

Examples of both exemplary and deplorable action will appear in the subsequent discussion, which draws freely on personal experiences, as well as my previous writings, reworked to provide a unified presentation.

Here are my sources:

The Eclipse of Excellence: A Critique of American Higher Education. Washington, D.C.: Public Affairs Press, 1973. Reprinted in 2004 by Wipf and Stock.

Education and the Democratic Ideal. Chicago: Nelson Hall, 1979. Reprinted in 2004 by Wipf and Stock.

Saints and Scamps: Ethics in Academia. Lanham, Md.: Rowman and Littlefield, 1986. Rev. ed., 1994. 25th anniversary ed., 2011.

Puzzles & Perplexities: Collected Essays. Lanham, Md.: Rowman and Littlefield, 2002. 2nd ed. 2007.

From Student to Scholar: A Candid Guide to Becoming a Professor. New
York: Columbia University Press, 2008.
Teaching Philosophy: A Guide. New York: Routledge, 2018.

I am grateful to my editor Lisa Banning for her continuing support, and to manuscript editor Ashley Moore for her conscientiousness. My brother, Victor L. Cahn, read every paragraph, offering sound advice on content as well as innumerable stylistic suggestions. To my wife, Marilyn Ross, M.D., I owe more than I would try to put into words.

Inside Academia

1

How Professors View Academia

In 1968, when I was appointed to the faculty at New York University, one of my first assignments was to teach a large section of Introductory Philosophy. The class had over one hundred students, and the huge room in which we met had both a back door, where most of the students entered, and a front door, where I came in. Those two doors symbolized for me the different perspectives of students and faculty members.

Many of the former come to college assuming that, as in elementary or high school, they are the primary focus of attention. Their supposition is that how they perform in the classroom is crucial to academic life, and that the grades they receive are of deep concern to their teachers.

The faculty, however, take a different view. For them, scholarly pursuit comes first, while any class is secondary. They consider research to be the core of the academic enterprise. Other activities on campus, whether involving students, administrators, or staff, are peripheral, important only insofar as they contribute to the faculty's efforts to achieve professional advancement.

This goal is typically pursued by publishing in professional journals, authoring or editing books with university presses and similar publishers, participating in academic conferences, and presenting lectures at colleges or universities. Such activities help build a strong academic reputation, leading to more prestigious invitations, appointments, and honors.

Even faculty members who have few academic accomplishments regard themselves as experts whose pursuit of knowledge, whether by writing, reading, or thinking, is the essence of academia. Although they may never complete any research, when asked about scholarly projects, they always claim to be working on one. Only a neophyte would admit, "I don't have any." Indeed, scholarship is recognized as so important that if a faculty member is asked to take on a departmental or institutional responsibility, the one negative reply that is invariably accepted runs along these lines: "I'd be happy to help, but I have an article I need to finish." That explanation points to a duty that supersedes all others.

When asked by a stranger what they do for a living, professors identify themselves not as teachers but as physicists, economists, literary critics, and so on. Their primary commitment is to their discipline, not their classes.

Indeed, few faculty members would not welcome a reduction in their instructional hours, known in the jargon as a "load." Research, incidentally, is never referred to as a "load" but as an "opportunity." Thus a professor might tell colleagues, "Good news. My teaching load has been reduced, so I'll finally have time for my own work."

Of course, faculty depend for their salaries on tuition dollars, but this reliance on the presence of students is of minor concern to professors. After all, teaching and advising students take away from time better spent on the faculty's own specializations.

How do faculty view the administration? While deans and provosts usually have high salaries and large offices, the faculty typically consider them subsidiary, former full-time professors whose scholarship may have tailed off but who have volunteered to think in an orderly manner about institutional policies. To be sure, they oversee budgets and enforce regulations, but their activity is not considered the heart of the academic enterprise. Indeed, their success is viewed as dependent almost entirely on whether they make life run smoothly for the faculty.

Presidents, on the other hand, come from any walk of life, whether law, business, politics, the military, or academia. Frequently they lack significant scholarly accomplishments that would give them standing with the faculty. Instead they possess the ambition and demeanor to be the voice of the institution. They look outward toward the community and government rather than inward toward the faculty and students. Although usually having only limited participation in the inner workings of academia, they are regarded by the public as crucial to life at their schools. Yet because they often have little impact on scholarly work, their presence may be barely noted by the faculty.

As for staff, they range from those involved in admissions, financial aid, and fund-raising, to administrative assistants, campus police, and maintenance personnel. While some of these people possess a deep understanding of their school and have devoted many years to its well-being, they are viewed by the faculty as merely supporting players, useful perhaps, but not essential.

The overall outlook of the faculty is captured in a story told about future president of the United States General Dwight D. Eisenhower when for a brief time he was president of Columbia University. At a ceremony welcoming faculty members back after summer break, he repeatedly referred to them as workers at the university. Finally, the

Nobel Prize–winning physicist I. I. Rabi spoke out: "Please, General, do not address us as if we were *employees* of the university—we *are* the university."[1] To grasp that comment is to understand how the faculty see themselves and their institutions.

2

Graduate School

Why do so many faculty members share the same viewpoint on academia? Because they all attended graduate schools that convey the same advice: specialize, publish in professional journals, and do not be distracted by other demands.

From the day first-year students go to graduate departmental orientation, they are asked about their planned specialization. The one reply sure to elicit guffaws from the faculty is: "I hope to become a teacher." After all, luminaries publish; only lightweights merely teach.

A corollary is that while publishing is hard, teaching is supposed to be easy. As a faculty member once wrote to me, "Most new PhDs seem to be able to get the hang of teaching after a few semesters." Only someone who attended graduate school would treat teaching in so cavalier a fashion.

Would anyone suppose that after a few semesters you could "get the hang" of teaching a large class of eighth graders the essentials of algebra, French grammar, or Shakespeare? The difficulties are so daunting that many who try are soon ready to quit in frustration. Why, then, would someone suppose that teaching physics, Russian literature, or philosophy to college students is easier? That view is a graduate school dogma, designed to downplay the skill and effort needed.

After all, if teaching is hard, then success would require concentrated practice, which would in turn take away from scholarship. Furthermore, teaching in graduate school would also be demanding, implying that instructors there have to think about pedagogy. Yet few do.

Indeed, the graduate level is where students are most likely to be subjected to neglect or mistreatment. The overall message is clear: teaching does not matter.

Here, for example, is a story told to me by an unimpeachable witness who took a course from a prolific scholar at one of the country's leading graduate schools. This professor had originally distributed a syllabus, but as the semester went on, he fell further behind schedule. With three weeks remaining, he explained the problem to the class: "There's no way we're going to be able to finish all the books I had hoped we would." At this point the class expected him to shorten the list, but he had a different solution in mind: "Why don't we just cancel the rest of the classes?" And he did. The irony is that given the quality of his teaching, no one objected.

Many graduate teachers have found a variety of ways to discharge their pedagogical duties relatively effortlessly. One method is to teach courses that are extensions of the professor's own research. That approach works because professors are allowed to announce topics of their choice, and the resulting conglomeration becomes the curriculum. The list may be unbalanced or of little use to those preparing for their careers, but such concerns are viewed as irrelevant.

For example, if a graduate professor is doing research on the German philosopher Eduard von Hartmann (1842–1906), a comparatively neglected figure in the history of philosophy, the professor could announce as a proposed course "The Philosophy of Eduard von Hartmann." Of course, students would most likely derive greater use from a course on Kant, Hegel, or Nietzsche, because those philosophers are taught far more often to undergraduates, but the Hartmann scholar would probably ignore that consideration. The strategy would almost surely fail, however, because few, if any, students would enroll in a Hartmann course, thus leading to its cancellation.

Others try a more sophisticated approach. One professor of musicology I knew was at work analyzing *Die Feen* (*The Fairies*), the earliest opera by Richard Wagner, unperformed in his lifetime and rarely produced. The professor, however, announced his course topic as Wagner's operas. Many students enrolled, only to discover that the entire semester was devoted to *Die Feen*. Why did students not complain? Because in graduate school no student wants to offend a professor who may later be in a position to help or hinder a career.

Another strategy for the reluctant teacher is to find a department member willing to offer a team-taught course. The work is shared, and each professor has the luxury of turning classes into conversations with a colleague. If even this device is too demanding, a professor can invite other scholars from inside or outside the school to lead discussions. Such a colloquium can be framed as offering students the opportunity to hear different points of view, but the actual result is even less work for the professor supposedly teaching the course.

If such a joint approach is not feasible, professors can still avoid teaching by distributing chapters from one of their own manuscripts, then assigning students to help edit it. Is such work the best way to learn a field? The question does not even arise, because the motivation for the professor is to pursue research while fulfilling a pedagogical obligation.

When all other stratagems fail, members of a department can appoint each other to quasi-administrative positions, then claim that these assignments entitle them to be released from at least some teaching. Consider these titles, devised by one graduate program: executive officer, deputy executive officer, director of graduate studies, placement officer, qualifying paper coordinator, colloquium coordinator, and two climate advisers. I am not sure who is supposed to need advice about the climate, but I am reminded of the positions held by the pompous Pooh-Bah in Gilbert and Sullivan's *The Mikado*: "First Lord of the Treasury, Lord Chief Justice, Commander-in-Chief, Lord High Admiral, Master of the Buckhounds, Groom of the Back Stairs, Archbishop of Titipu, and Lord Mayor, both acting and elect." You may wonder how many students this program admits each year. About a dozen. And the number is intentionally kept small, so that professors will not be burdened with too many students to teach or advise.

Even when a graduate instructor teaches a standard course in a standard way, the results are often unsatisfactory. The tendency is to toss out names, terms, and concepts regardless of whether everyone is familiar with them. One result is that students are cowed into hiding their lack of knowledge and developing the unfortunate trait of pretending to know what they do not, leaving them defenseless against others who engage in obfuscation.

That weakness explains the results of a famous psychological study known as the "Doctor Fox" experiment.[1] A distinguished-looking professional actor with an authoritative manner was selected to present a lecture to several groups of educators. They were told they would be hearing a talk by Dr. Myron L. Fox, an expert on the application of mathematics to human behavior. His address was titled "Mathematical Game Theory as Applied to Physician Education." The actor was coached "to present his topic and conduct his question-and-answer period with an excessive use of double talk, neologies, non sequiturs, and contradictory statements. All this was to be interspersed with parenthetical and meaningless references to unrelated topics."

At the end of the one-hour lecture and subsequent half-hour discussion, a questionnaire was distributed to the listeners, inquiring what they thought of Dr. Fox. Here are some responses:

Excellent presentation, enjoyed listening.
Has warm manner. Good flow, seems enthusiastic.
Lively examples. Extremely articulate.
Good analysis of subject that has been personally studied before.
He was certainly captivating. Knowledgeable.

My favorite reply was offered by one participant who found the presentation "too intellectual." Most important, all the listeners had many more favorable than unfavorable responses, and not one saw through the hoax.

Why not? Because graduate students have been taught the importance of always appearing knowledgeable. Their guiding principle: ignorance is ignominious. As a result, graduate students become reluctant to ask elementary questions and instead nod knowingly even when a supposed expert is misguiding them. Such passivity is especially unfortunate because graduate professors so often fail to observe principles of good pedagogy, and their presentations frequently are bewildering, even disheartening.

The situation was captured in the true story of a graduate student taking the last course required for his degree, a class taught by an illustrious scholar in a different department. At a break during the initial session, another student leaned over and remarked, "I just began here. Are all the courses so boring?" To which the first replied, "You bet. In fact, this is the most interesting one I've taken."

On an autobiographical note, I have to say that the first two classes I attended in graduate school left me similarly dismayed. In the first, our professor, whose presentation was hard to follow, explained that in subsequent weeks we would be reading one book per class, and a student would be assigned to lead each discussion (yet another common strategy to avoid the responsibilities of teaching). Every student was asked to choose a book, but no one volunteered for the one the professor described as especially demanding, and he became visibly angry. To everyone's relief, I offered to take on the assignment. A little while later, however, I realized that the course was bound to be trouble, and I dropped it (although I did feel sorry for whichever unfortunate classmate was stuck presenting a talk on the difficult volume I had abandoned).

Although the instructor in my second class was more amiable, the session itself was no better. He had written an important work on the subject he was teaching, so I anticipated that his lectures would be enlightening. Unfortunately, they consisted of nothing more than his reading his book out loud, word for word. As you might expect, I dropped that course as well.

I was registered for only one more course and entered that class anticipating that my stint as a graduate student might soon end. Yet within two hours, my life changed, and I was on my way to a professorial career.

3

Turning Point

Teachers can be an enormous force for good or ill. Indeed, they may have far more impact on the many students they meet than on the few scholars who may read their journal articles. Having already described professors who left me dispirited, I turn now to the one who gave me the inspiration to embrace a calling.

I should explain that when I enrolled as a graduate student in Columbia University's Department of Philosophy, I was unsure that I was taking the right step and wondered whether I ought instead to have been pursuing other long-standing interests by embarking on a doctoral program in American history, attending law school, or studying piano at a conservatory.

As I looked through the semester's offerings, I came upon a course titled "Philosophical Analysis." I had no idea what it was about and was unfamiliar with the instructor, Richard Taylor, who had recently come to Columbia from Brown University, but, following a suggestion from the graduate adviser, I enrolled.

Shortly before the announced time, I entered the department's luxurious seminar room, sat in one of the plush chairs, and, surrounded by many other students, anticipated the appearance of our professor. When he arrived, he began by telling us that this course would be different from others we might have taken. We would not study the writings of famous philosophers of the past or pore over learned commentaries about them. Rather, we would *do* philosophy. We would not read about philosophers; we would ourselves *be* philosophers. Having spent many undergraduate hours struggling with knotty works written centuries before, and given my discouraging experience so far in graduate school, I welcomed whatever he had in mind.

He informed us that the reading for the course would consist of only a few articles, and that we would be writing three papers in which we ourselves tried to solve the very issues discussed in those articles. I found this plan hard to believe. Bertrand Russell or John Dewey might solve a philosophical problem, but how could I? After all, I had just started graduate school and had read only some of the classics. How could I solve a philosophical problem? And who would be interested in reading my views?

Professor Taylor next told us that the first article we were to discuss had not yet appeared in print. This announcement added to my surprise, because I had never read a professional article prior to publication. He proceeded to distribute mimeographed pages by a scholar unknown to me. Our assignment, we were told, was to analyze this essay and decide whether its main contention was correct.

Professor Taylor then approached the chalkboard, wrote several statements, and asked whether the last statement followed from the previous ones.

A student raised his hand and launched into a speech full of technical terms and references to the works of several medieval thinkers. As Professor Taylor listened intently, his face expressed first hope, then disappointment. "I'm afraid I don't understand much of what you said," he replied. "I didn't ask anything about any medieval philosophers. I asked only if the last statement is implied by the previous ones. What do you think?" The student shrugged and looked frustrated.

Another student confidently raised her hand and inquired whether the issue had not been handled adequately in an article that had appeared many years before in a leading philosophical journal. Professor Taylor responded, "I really don't know. I haven't read that article. But perhaps you can tell us: Is the last sentence implied by the previous ones?" The student replied that she could not remember. "But," he continued, "there's nothing to remember. The statements are on the board. Does the last follow from the others, or doesn't it?" She offered no reply.

Never in my study of philosophy had I witnessed such an approach. I was unfamiliar with the medieval thinkers to whom the first student had referred, and I knew nothing of the article to which the second student had alluded. The answer to the professor's question, however, was not to be found in a dog-eared tome or a dusty journal. We were being asked to think, to philosophize.

Suddenly I understood what Professor Taylor had meant when he said we would try to solve philosophical problems, and at that moment I experienced a remarkable liberation. I raised my hand and presented my opinion, something I had been reluctant to do in other classes, for fear that my incomplete command of philosophical literature would be apparent to all. Professor Taylor indicated that my comment was intriguing but inquired how I would deal with a certain objection. I was unsure and sat silently, pondering. By the time an answer came to me, the class was over.

I decided to visit him and pursue my point. Other professors were usually available for conferences with students only three or four hours a week. Professor Taylor met with his students three or four *afternoons* a week—for several hours each afternoon. I was accustomed to waiting in line to see a popular teacher, but Professor Taylor placed a sheet on his office door so students could sign up in advance for fifteen- or thirty-minute appointments.

The next day, I ventured in and began presenting my ideas. Before long, though, he interrupted: "Write a paper for me." I had not intended to write down my views, believing that I needed only to communicate them orally, but he made clear that putting ideas into writing was indispensable to precise thinking.

I returned home, worked harder than I could remember, and the following week brought him a paper. He told me he would read it and get back to me. Several days later, eager to learn his reaction, I knocked on his door before the announced office hours and timidly inquired whether he had read my essay. He replied that he was busy writing and could not speak further with me but would return the paper. He passed it through the half-open door and said he would see me later. On the front page was his comment, the substance of which was that after further work, the paper ought to be published, then serve as a section of my dissertation.

I was stunned. Here I was in my first month of graduate study and had been told not only that I had written something worth publishing but that I had already, in essence, completed part of my dissertation.

For the next two years I devoted myself to justifying his confidence. I attended every class he taught and wrote paper after paper. I signed up for conferences with him several times a week and often waited near his office to take advantage of free time created by the cancellation of a scheduled appointment. He never begrudged me a moment but continued urging me to write more and come to discuss what I had written. The hours we spent together became the focus of my life.

I no longer doubted my choice of career, and through his patience and efforts I became a philosopher. Incidentally, his reaction to that first paper proved prophetic, because three years after writing it, I received my PhD, and my dissertation included the already-published material from that initial piece.

Richard Taylor died years ago, but whenever I think about the responsibilities of a teacher, I remember with deep gratitude his invaluable guidance that enabled me to overcome my misgivings and find my way through the world of academia. I only wish every graduate student might be so fortunate.

4

How Teachers Succeed

Not only was Richard Taylor a superb teacher of philosophy in both graduate and undergraduate settings, he was one of the world's foremost authorities on apiculture, the science of beekeeping. Indeed, his numerous books and articles on that subject were considered models of instruction. Thus his skill at teaching did not depend on his topic or audience. What, then, explains his success and that of others who excel in the art of leading students to master a subject while arousing appreciation for it, yet neither misrepresenting nor diluting it?

To grasp the challenge, imagine trying to explain baseball to a person unfamiliar with the sport. Where would you begin? With the roles of the pitcher and catcher? How about the calling of balls and strikes? Or the location of the bases, how to score runs, or the ways outs can be made? The fundamental difficulty is that all these starting points presume knowledge of some of the others. How, then, can you break the circle of intertwining concepts and make the subject accessible?

Now imagine teaching a class in calculus, English history, or Chinese. Any of these subjects is far more complex than baseball. Moreover, rather than a single listener, a class contains many students with varying skills, interests, and backgrounds. Thus reaching the entire group is a major challenge.

My point is that teaching is hard. Even with a thorough understanding of a subject, conveying that knowledge can be frustrating for all involved. Yet some instructors succeed to an amazing degree.

Now the crucial question: What do these teachers have in common that others lack?

The answer is *not* that successful teachers know the subject better than others. Rather, they have mastered pedagogical skills that, surprising to some, are the same whether the students are children, teenagers, or adults.

Show me a terrific fifth-grade teacher, and I will show you someone who, with some specialist study, could become an outstanding instructor at the collegiate level. Show me a boring college professor, and I will show you someone who would be equally tiresome to a class of ten-year-olds.

One difference, however, is that those ten-year-olds faced with an ineffective instructor will probably yell or throw things, while poorly taught college students will simply fall asleep.

But what are the fundamentals of pedagogic success? The essence is contained in three strategic steps.

The first is commonly referred to as motivation. Without it, a class stagnates. After all, how long will you watch a movie that does nothing to capture your attention? Or read a novel that begins with a situation of no interest? The slower the start, the more difficult to generate enthusiasm. At best, the audience allows you a few minutes without much action. The same with teaching.

Consider the openings of the following two lectures, delivered in the years 1970 and 1969 as the presidential addresses of the Eastern Division Meeting of the American Philosophical Association. Each was presented to an audience consisting of approximately five hundred philosophers.

One speaker was the eminent American philosopher Wilfrid Sellars, who taught at the University of Pittsburgh. He began as follows: "The quotation which I have taken as my text occurs in the opening paragraphs of the Paralogisms of Pure Reason in which Kant undertakes a critique of what he calls 'Rational Psychology.' The paragraphs are common to the two editions of the *Critique of Pure Reason*, and the formulations they contain may be presumed to have continued to satisfy him—at least as introductory remarks."[1] If your interest in reading further is minimal, many in the audience shared that attitude, for although the subject matter was relevant to Kant scholars, not one word Sellars offered motivated his other listeners.

What could he have done instead?

One answer is found in the address given a year earlier by the renowned British philosopher Stuart Hampshire, who was then teaching at Princeton University. He, too, wished to give an exposition of a text but offered a far more provocative opening: "I want to speak today about a philosophy of mind to which I will not at first assign an identity or date, except that its author could not have lived and worked before 1600. He is modern, in the sense that he thinks principally about the future applications of the physical sciences to the study of personality. As I speak, I hope that it will not at first be too easy for you to tell whether or not he is our contemporary, whether indeed he is not present in this room. I attempt this reconstruction as a way of praising a philosopher who has not, I think, been at all justly interpreted so far."[2]

Hampshire's withholding the name of the author was a brilliant stroke, because members of the audience were immediately curious as to whom he was referring. As they looked around, wondering if the subject was there, they also listened carefully, treating Hampshire's every sentence as a clue. Finally, a few minutes from his conclusion, Hampshire revealed that the author in question was Baruch Spinoza (1632–1677) and ended by quoting the passage from Spinoza's *Ethics* that had been the unspoken focus.

Had Hampshire begun by quoting the text he intended to discuss, the philosophical substance would have been unchanged, but doing so would have been a pedagogical disaster, for few would have listened with special care. But by making his talk a puzzle, Hampshire captivated his audience, and, having been present myself, I can testify that the quiet in the hall was striking.

Hampshire's talk was no richer philosophically than that of Sellars. But, pedagogically speaking, their two lectures were of vastly different quality.

Here is another example of effective motivation, coming not from the acme of the scholarly world but from a far more ordinary setting. The description is offered by my brother, Victor L. Cahn, now professor emeritus of English at Skidmore College, who earlier in his career was a highly successful preparatory school teacher.[3] His first experience in that milieu took place at Mercersberg Academy in Pennsylvania. When he arrived as a novice, he observed a veteran instructor teaching vocabulary to a class of ten high school juniors. No one, instructor or students, was engrossed by the activity.

The next day, my brother was asked to take over the group. At first he began calling on the boys, much as his colleague had done, and asking them to define words. But he soon realized that the students were bored, and so was he.

Here, in his own words, is what happened.

After a timid answer from one student, I challenged the next: "Do you agree with that definition?"

"Yes."

"Are you sure?"

"I think so."

My eyebrows rose in feigned disbelief. "But I sense doubt. And our only way of resolving the uncertainty is to solicit another opinion."

As I began to fire questions around the room, the company before me sat up straight and began to grin. Gradually I became more animated, almost like a vaudevillian comic peppering the audience with one-liners. I heard myself call for words to be used in sentences, for two words to be used in the same sentence, for students to quiz each other, for ever more complicated routines and games.

In the meantime I maintained a cheerful patter. "Bravo! And if I claimed to be 'abstemious,' would I be more or less rigorous in my self-denial than if I was 'ascetic'?"

And to the next: "Jack, would you consider that definition 'apt' or unnecessarily 'abstruse'? And, if so, why? And, if not, why not?"

And later . . .

"Bob, I see that we're nearing the end of this portion of the entertainment. I presume that leaves you feeling acrimonious."

"No, sir," with a smile.

"What do you mean, 'No, sir'? Are you implying that I have mischaracterized your mood?"

"I don't know, but you're using the wrong word," with a snicker.

My face registered shock. "Am I to understand that you have the temerity to correct my usage?"

"That's what I'm doing."

By now everyone was chuckling. "Allen, I see you find all this amusing. Then you must agree with Bob."

"He nailed you, sir!"

"But 'acrimonious' means 'pleased,' doesn't it?

"Not even close. It means 'bitter.'"

"Scott, he's correcting me! Can you believe that?"

"Yes, sir."

"And can you think of a word that would describe his boldness in doing so?"

"How about 'audacious'?"

I continued in this manner for nearly half an hour, until everyone in the room was breathless.

My brother's account profits from his being a playwright with numerous off-Broadway productions to his credit, but his strategy in that classroom offers several important pedagogic insights.

First, he was conscious of the tedium caused by his initial presentation. Too many unsuccessful teachers are unaware or uncaring of their impact on students. These instructors often ascribe a boring class to the students rather than the pedagogy.

On the contrary, when my brother realized the situation, he picked up the pace, injected humor, and turned the class into a sort of show. By involving the students in the learning process and having them use key words in sentences not just in isolation, he deepened their understanding while enhancing their enthusiasm.

In this case the motivational device was the style in which the material was presented, as well as the personality of the instructor. That my brother has an ingratiating sense of humor surely benefits his teaching, but laughter in the classroom needs to be put in the service of learning, not treated as an end in itself. Yet if the instructor has a winning personality and can rely on it to interest students in the subject, so much the better.

I hasten to add, however, that successful teaching in a classroom does not require a lively demeanor outside it. In this regard I recall my experience at the Colby College Summer School of Languages, begun with Swarthmore College in 1948 but in 1955 becoming exclusively a Colby program, highly regarded until disbanded for financial reasons in 1968. Four languages were offered—French, German, Russian, and Spanish—each at the introductory, intermediate, and advanced levels. At meals, only the foreign language was spoken, and in the evening, cultural programs such as foreign-language films and lectures on classical music were offered. Outstanding instructors from various colleges participated, and I may have established a record by attending three times to study three different languages: Russian to meet a college language requirement, then French and German for my doctorate.

At the end of my stint with French, I told friends who had been studying German there that I planned to return the next summer to take on that language myself. Immediately they urged me to enroll in the section of grammar taught by Philip Bither, a graduate of Colby who had served on its faculty throughout his career. Having seen him around campus, I was perplexed by the recommendation. Professor Bither was a quiet man who sought and attracted little attention. Why would I want to face a dull fellow teaching a dull subject?

Nevertheless, when the next summer arrived, I requested that he admit me to his section. He casually signed the necessary paper, but I remained apprehensive.

In the building where we met, bells indicated the beginning and end of classes, so on the first day I sat with a dozen other students awaiting the instructor and the signal. Soon Professor Bither appeared, inexpressive as always.

Then the bell rang.

At once Professor Bither turned into a whirlwind, speaking quickly and decisively. As he rapidly went from student to student posing questions from our textbook, he compelled us to reply at his speed, not our own. If a student answered correctly, Professor Bither surprised us again. He did not move to the next student, a familiar pattern that encourages not listening to answers but looking ahead to figure out which question you will be asked. Instead he responded to the student who had answered correctly, "Good, take the next one." Then, after another correct answer, "Good, take another." The pace was frenetic. Finally, when everyone was exhausted, the bell rang, and Professor Bither resumed his quiet demeanor and ambled out.

In sum, the course was unforgettable. I enjoyed learning German grammar but never again supposed I could predict how someone I had met outside a classroom would perform within it.

I should add that many years later, while teaching at the University of Vermont, I was waiting for a bus one wintry day when a member of the German department joined me. Seeking a topic I thought might enliven the bleakness of the afternoon, I mentioned that one summer I had studied German at Colby College with Professor Philip Bither and inquired whether my colleague knew him. As it turned out, he did, but expressed consolation at what he presumed had been my boredom. As the bus arrived and I was boarding, I looked back and said that, on the contrary, Professor Bither's classes were among the most exciting I had ever experienced. My colleague's face expressed sheer incredulity, as he wondered how the Philip Bither he knew could have taught an interesting course, or how I could have had such a strange reaction.

In Professor Bither's case, his style was the motivation. Few, however, can adopt such a passionate approach, but even attempting to arouse interest will likely involve some students, who might well follow where the teacher leads.

Yet even with a motivated student, a successful teacher needs to know how to take advantage of such interest. Which brings us to the second key strategy: organization, presenting material in a sequence that promotes understanding.

Previously I discussed trying to teach the rules of baseball to someone unfamiliar with the sport. Consider offering the following explanation:

"In playing baseball, you try to score runs. Only the team to whom the ball is pitched can score. You run around the bases and try to avoid outs. Four balls result in walks. The game has nine innings."

This attempted instruction is a fiasco—not that any of the statements is false. Each is true yet not only disconnected from the previous ones but also presuming knowledge the listener does not possess.

The first statement refers to "runs," but the learner has not been told how a run is scored. The second statement refers to a ball being "pitched," but the role of the pitcher has not been explained. The remaining statements refer to "bases," "outs," "balls," "walks," and "innings," but none of these terms has been put in context, so that if you do not already understand baseball, you will not learn anything. In other words, a presentation can be factual yet not pedagogically well organized.

Imagine another experience, common in the days before cars were equipped with GPS, of driving through an unfamiliar town trying to find the highway. You ask directions from a passerby, who responds, "It's easy. Just turn right as you approach the supermarket, then turn left at the second light before the firehouse, then turn right at the stop sign near the post office, and you can't miss it." The problem is obvious: If you are a stranger and do not know where the landmarks are, how can you know when to turn?

Poor teachers may not care whether their students understand a presentation, but successful teachers are eager to explain basic points to those who have trouble grasping them. An instructor who gripes about the need to offer such help is akin to a surgeon who complains that the patients are sick.

Every student making an effort to learn should have the opportunity to do so. That aim can be achieved, however, only if material is presented in an effective order.

How can it be achieved? My suggestion would be to start by planning. You have to ask yourself whether your first substantive remark will be understood by those with no prior knowledge of the subject. If so, how about the second, third, and fourth? Will everyone be able to follow your train of thought? That standard is tough, but it is part of why teaching is demanding.

Even a well-organized presentation, however, will not succeed if the material is not presented with clarity, the third key strategy.

A basic problem is speaking too quickly. No matter what your content, if your delivery is overly fast, you will not be understood. Indeed, the most obvious sign of a poor lecturer is rushing. When those who are inexperienced come to a podium, they hardly ever speak at a proper pace. Yet when you hear a genuine orator, the sentences are never hurried. No student will ever object to your speaking too slowly, but many will complain if the words cascade too quickly.

Another problem is using terminology the audience does not understand. If I remark that for a year I worked at the NEH, which has a different mission from the NEA and is unconnected to the DOJ, Washington insiders will know that I am referring to the National Endowment for the

Humanities, the National Endowment for the Arts, and the Department of Justice, but others will be lost. Should they know these acronyms? Maybe; maybe not. Either way, if many are unfamiliar with them, that is reason enough not to use them without explanation.

Imagine listening to an instructor in an introductory course who says, "To paraphrase the author of *The Pastorals*, a sparse supply of cognition is a minatory entity." Few in any class are likely to understand this remark. If the problem is pointed out to the speaker, the irritated reply may be, "It's obvious I'm referring to Alexander Pope." "But who," a student might ask, "is Alexander Pope?" At this point the instructor is likely to burst out with frustration: "How can you not know?" Perhaps needless to say, this person is not cut out to be a teacher. And even if the students were told that Pope was a celebrated eighteenth-century English poet, they probably still would not realize that the teacher was paraphrasing Pope's line, "A little learning is a dangerous thing," which, in fact, may itself be unknown to many.

And why use the word "minatory"? Hardly anyone will be familiar with its meaning, which is derived from the Latin word *minari*, meaning, "to threaten." Yet inept teachers proceed in such confusing ways all the time.

Another reason for lack of clarity is omitting steps in reasoning. Suppose an instructor of first-year students who need to brush up on algebra says, "Given that $17 - 11 = 3x$, we know that $2x = 4$." Many students in the class will not follow the reasoning. The teacher has failed to take the time to explain how the first equation proves that $x = 2$, and thus that $2 \times 2 = 4$.

The teacher might respond that such reasoning is obvious. Well, it may be obvious to the teacher but not to all the students, and their understanding should be the teacher's focus.

But can you not omit what seems apparent? The question brings to mind an incident, reported by a number of witnesses, involving Willard Van Orman Quine, one of the greatest logicians of the twentieth century and a professor of philosophy at Harvard University. His textbook on symbolic logic was widely used, and although he did not relish teaching the subject, he was occasionally asked to do so. Once in such a course, after he wrote a proof on the board, a student raised his hand and asked impatiently, "Why bother writing out that proof? It's obvious." To which Quine replied, "Young man, this entire course is obvious."

In an introductory class, everything taught may be obvious—obvious to the teacher but not to the students. The same may sometimes be true even in a graduate seminar.

To sum up, when you discover a teacher who motivates the class, organizes the material, and presents it clearly, you have found an effective instructor. And whether the class is composed of fifth graders, high schoolers, undergraduates, or PhD candidates, the same principles apply.

Few individuals have taught at all these levels, but one who did was as successful a teacher as I have ever known, a philosophy professor at New York University named Robert Gurland. While his colleagues would teach ten or twenty students in a course, he would, whatever the subject, always teach over two hundred. On the first day of registration, his classes filled, and the demand invariably far exceeded the number of seats. Regardless of gender, race, ethnicity, or level of philosophical sophistication, students wanted to enroll, and even some who failed his course sought to take it again with him. He reciprocated the students' passion by knowing the name of everyone in every class, learning something about each, and personally grading, with detailed comments, every one of their hundreds of papers. Coincidentally, two highly successful philosophy professors I formerly taught, one a man, the other a woman, both took multiple undergraduate courses with Professor Gurland and decades later remain immensely grateful to him.

Admittedly, he had a most engaging personality, a wonderful sense of humor, and an unusual background that included stints as a minor league baseball player and a professional trumpeter in leading jazz bands, experiences that provided him with a plethora of amusing anecdotes. When, however, I asked him to explain his success, he opened his briefcase and held up stacks of yellow pads filled with writing. He explained that these were his lectures, and although he never looked at them during his classes, he knew exactly what material he was going to cover and how it would be presented. Even his vivid examples were written down. In short, his seemingly freewheeling style was carefully plotted.

What may be surprising is that Professor Gurland began as an elementary school teacher of mathematics and science, then taught those subjects in junior high school and high school, then taught college mathematics and philosophy, and finally was asked to teach logic to graduate school students. Although he won teaching awards at a variety of levels, I doubt he cared much what group he was asked to instruct. (On several occasions he taught courses at West Point and was an enormous hit with the cadets.) He was simply a teacher, bringing his vast pedagogical skills to every classroom he entered.

Looking back on your school years, you are apt to remember only a few instructors who deepened your understanding of a subject while also enhancing your appreciation of it. I need not wonder whether they offered motivation, organization, and clarity. Surely, like all those I have mentioned by name, they did.

5

Teaching Graduate Students to Teach

Can anything be done to change how faculty members view teaching? I believe so, but a multifaceted approach is needed.

A primary step is to require that all graduate students who seek a faculty position participate in a departmental colloquium that prepares them for offering effective instruction to undergraduates. For many years I offered such a credit-bearing course in the Philosophy Program at the City University of New York Graduate Center, and the results were dramatic.

While some class time was spent discussing ethical obligations and pedagogic principles, as well as developing sample syllabi and examinations, most of the hours were devoted to practice. Each of the approximately fifteen students gave a series of short presentations to the class, after which the speaker received immediate feedback from me and the other students. If, during the talk, someone did not understand a term the speaker had used, that listener would immediately raise a hand, thereby requesting an explanation.

At first, most of the participants were nervous as they stood before the audience. They mumbled, talked too fast, laughed self-consciously, and stared at the ceiling, the chalkboard, or their notes, avoiding eye contact with those they were supposed to be addressing. They made little attempt to interest their listeners in the subject. They used technical terms without explaining them, thus provoking numerous raised hands. They became lost in minutiae. In short, these beginners displayed all the pedagogical short-comings that turn too many college classrooms into scenes of apathy and confusion.

But whereas most instructors who communicate inade-quately are never called to account, in this case weak presen-tations brought forth a series of constructive suggestions. Not only did these help the speaker, but they reinforced for all participants the elements of sound instruction and the pre-cautions needed to avoid pedagogic pitfalls.

Soon noticeable improvements occurred. The students began to speak more slowly, motivate their audience, and organize the talks so that ideas were presented in a compre-hensible sequence. Fewer hands were raised. Most remark-ably, some students whose initial stage fright had made them seem somber or remote turned out, after becoming more at ease, to be engaging and even humorous.

Students whose presentations showed marked improve-ment received generous plaudits from the others, and the developing esprit de corps encouraged all to try to enhance their performance. Before long, most of the talks were more compelling, and the students who continued to struggle at least were conscious of the reasons for their lack of success.

After listening to each of the final presentations, all the students wrote evaluations that I later shared anonymously at personal conferences with each member of the class. Per-haps I can convey most effectively what we accomplished by quoting a sampling of these comments, each condensed but using the exact words of a respondent.

- Energetic, attention-grabbing, and polished presentation. Nice motivation, leading expertly to the topic to be discussed. Smooth interaction with students; handled comments well without distraction. Clear exposition of the issues at hand. Should avoid using notes too much. Should slow down a bit.

- Way too many "OKs." Too much looking at the board. No attempt at motivation. Many opportunities for discussion passed over. Though he asked us to raise our hands if we had a comment, there didn't seem to be any opportunities to do so.

- Powerful example used to motivate interest. The pace at times was a bit fast, perhaps because of nervousness. You asked questions but mostly answered them yourself. I think this made for a certain disengagement on the part of the class. It's hard to hold interest by just talking to the class. You need to connect to them.

- Became much more comfortable toward the end, warmed up, relaxed. You became able to use emphasis and tone to create drama, suspense, and interest. Nice, personable manner, and slow, clear pace.

- Don't look at the board like you're expecting it to do something. Make sure you're making eye contact with us. Your tone is calm and reassuring. Great use of example to build the point. You use the class and their answers well. It becomes a fun discussion.

- The pacing was a little fast in some places. Examples worked well, but I think that discussing them further, especially by asking students to participate at some point, would have worked even better. Overall, a lively and interesting presentation of a difficult topic.

- There's no motivation, no gateway into the issue. Way too attached to notes. Put them down. We desperately need examples. There's too much terminology tossed about, and nothing relevant or playful to tie it down. The main thrust of your attention is the board. Make the students your primary focus.

- Considerably more comfortable and casual than in previous presentations. Good use of humor to engage audience. Much better job of making eye contact and connecting with the class. A lot of information is covered a little too quickly. It would be a good idea to use the board to set up and outline and keep track of key terms. But overall so much better. Congratulations!

Aspiring college teachers who took such a course would never again suppose that teaching is easy, and their efforts to master essential pedagogic techniques would pay off in more effective instruction. Granted, no course is likely to turn a poor teacher into a great one. However, if taken during those formative years of graduate study, when individuals are most likely to welcome help, the advice provided can turn inaudible, unclear, or disorganized speakers into audible, clear, and organized ones. Most important, it can turn thoughtless instructors into thoughtful ones, a crucial step on the path toward more effective and responsible teaching.

6

Changing Departmental Culture

To invest teaching with importance, offering a course for graduate students is helpful but not sufficient. Also needed are changes in departmental priorities and policies.

When an opening is announced, the description of the position should emphasize the importance of excellence in teaching. Because any criterion not specified originally ought not be used later, that stress needs to be present from the outset.

Too often the search takes teaching ability for granted, presuming that everyone who has earned an advanced degree can teach adequately. The goal, however, should not be adequacy but excellence.

While many letters of reference contain a sentence praising a candidate's pedagogical skills, the author usually lacks evidence to support such an assessment. Here is a typical comment: "I have never seen Smith teach, but knowing her well, I am sure she will be highly successful with students." If not based on classroom observation, such remarks should be discounted.

The importance of teaching is likely to be appreciated by graduate programs only if departments making an appointment publicize that their judgments will emphasize quality of instruction. If, for example, they announce that anyone who has taken a course in teaching will be viewed with more favor, graduate programs would be motivated to include such a class in the curriculum.

Furthermore, interviewers should not concentrate only on a candidate's doctoral dissertation and research plans but also ask questions such as: (1) If you were to teach an introductory course, what texts would you use, which issues would you cover, and how would you evaluate students? (2) How about the same information regarding a basic course in each area in which you claim competence? (3) What do you think of the practice of grading students, and how would you plan to approach this task? The answers would indicate how seriously a candidate regards teaching.

A common practice is requiring candidates to submit a statement describing their approach to teaching, but the information provided is rarely helpful. If you wanted to judge a violinist, would you do so on the basis of the performer's written statement? Surely not. You would, instead, want to hear the violinist play. Similarly, the key issue in evaluating candidates is not how elegantly they write but how effectively they teach.

For that reason, candidates invited for campus interviews should be expected to present both a research paper and a talk on an elementary topic, organized and presented as if for introductory students. Only those candidates whose classroom performance is proficient should be considered seriously. As anyone who has attended such a talk knows, a candidate's pedagogical ability quickly becomes obvious. Some individuals display the requisite skills, whereas others mumble and fumble. Just as those who cannot ably defend their research are passed over, the same fate should befall those who cannot ably teach.

Years ago when I chaired the Department of Philosophy at the University of Vermont, the head of the philosophy department at a large state university asked me whether at my school, like his, enrollment in philosophy courses had been shrinking. I told him that, on the contrary, ours had been growing. Amazed, he wondered how I accounted for this phenomenon.

"Excellent teaching," I said. "We try to make sure that everyone we appoint offers both first-rate scholarship and teaching. What do you look for?"

"Good scholars," he replied. "We never appoint anyone who hasn't delivered a scholarly paper."

"Why not test their teaching, too?" I inquired.

"Never thought of it," he muttered.

If a baseball team is comprised of strong hitters who are inadequate fielders, the result will be many hits and many errors. Likewise, if a department appoints strong researchers who are inadequate teachers, the result will be more papers published and fewer students enrolled.

Furthermore, just as new faculty members should be given permission to observe classes of senior members of the department, so new faculty members should occasionally be observed, not to be formally evaluated but to be offered suggestions where appropriate. Professors provide one another assistance in their writing; why should they not provide help in teaching as well?

We would view with suspicion a surgeon who barred all other surgeons from an operation. We should view with equal skepticism any professors who wish to lock classroom doors against knowledgeable observers.

Regarding decisions for promotion and tenure, departments currently care enough about research to undertake an elaborate review of scholarship. Similarly, departments ought to be concerned enough about teaching to undertake an equally elaborate review of a professor's work in the classroom. Such a review should involve input from departmental colleagues who visit the professor's classes and examine syllabi, examinations, and test papers to assess teaching performance.

Some suppose that students should have the strongest voice in evaluating a teacher, because they suffer the consequences of inadequate instruction. Yet this line of argument is fallacious. When airplane pilots fail to fulfill their obligations, passengers suffer the consequences, but passengers should not have a strong voice in evaluating pilots. Assuming, for example, that a plane has a rough landing, was the pilot at fault? Simply being a passenger does not enable one to know.

Admittedly, some instructors who receive unflattering student evaluations deserve them. Other instructors, however, can be victims of their own unyielding commitments to tough course requirements, demanding examinations, rigorous grading practices, or unfashionable intellectual positions. Because these factors and others requiring expertise in the subject may not be appreciated in student evaluations, heavy dependence on them menaces academic standards.

While some educational researchers agree that students can provide useful information, numerous studies confirm that student evaluations need to be considered in the context of peer evaluations. Otherwise, as one study concluded, departments are "flying blind."[1]

One final point: just as an outstanding researcher may be awarded tenure even with a weak performance in the classroom, so tenure should also be available to an outstanding teacher with a thin record of research. Granted, the ideal candidate excels as both researcher and teacher, but if an occasional exception is made so as not to lose a researcher of national stature, an occasional exception should also be made so as not to lose a teacher of extraordinary accomplishment.

Few teachers can attain such a level of excellence, but to oust one who does is shortsighted.

Doing so will also be unjust, because students pay a great deal for the privilege of attending classes. Any department that cares deeply about education will take all necessary steps to ensure that generations of students receive the first-rate instruction to which they are entitled.

7

The Administration

Even if faculty members do not place a high value on teaching, outside observers might suppose that administrators do. After all, ask presidents, provosts, or deans if they care deeply about the quality of instruction at their school, and they will assure you of their concern. Too often, however, their actions belie their words.

For instance, which candidate for a faculty position is viewed as more attractive: the promising researcher or the promising teacher? Whose requests for support carry greater weight? The answers are obvious. If administrators were as concerned about teaching as they say, their commitment would be demonstrated by policies different from those now in place.

First, when salary raises are distributed, excellence in teaching would be weighed as heavily as excellence in research. Granted, some institutions give teaching prizes to a select few while rewarding many for their research, but what remains unheard of is giving research prizes to a select few while rewarding many for their teaching.

Furthermore, just as faculty members are given release time to pursue their scholarship, so they would be eligible for release time to develop a new course or methodology. They would also be offered the opportunity to attend a teaching center, receiving guidance from master teachers to strengthen pedagogic skills.

In addition, those who care about teaching should recognize levels of effectiveness. All appreciate the differences between research that is incompetent, barely competent, mediocre, strong, or superb; the same distinctions apply to teaching. Not every sound researcher is a serious candidate for a Nobel Prize or its equivalent; neither is every sound teacher a serious candidate for a teaching hall of fame. Yet administrators, like faculty, show little interest in drawing such distinctions. Describing all teachers as "good" or "not so good" is a sign that teaching is not taken seriously. Even if an individual is said to be a good teacher, a key question is, How good? And what steps can be taken to improve even a fairly good performance?

Another indication of a lack of administrative interest in teaching is that while institutions sometimes seek to recruit a strong researcher to help a department increase its national visibility, I know of few, if any, schools that have recruited an outstanding teacher to enable a department to strengthen its offerings to students. Yet administrators committed to teaching would encourage departments to conduct such searches.

Why do administrators value a renowned researcher more highly than the best of instructors? If a school adds a nationally celebrated figure to its faculty, students who are considering attending the school, as well as parents and friends, will be impressed by the presence of such a notable. But has any prospective student ever chosen a school because its faculty members have a reputation for excellence in teaching? On the contrary, the belief is that by virtue of their positions, all professors will be effective in the classroom. That assumption, however, is not likely to survive even one semester of classes.

Beyond focusing attention on the institution, the productive scholar in the sciences, as well as the social sciences, attracts outside funding that contributes significantly to the school's coffers. On the other hand, a superb instructor does not necessarily generate funds and is at best a local celebrity: legendary, perhaps, on campus but likely unknown outside its gates.

Furthermore, if an administrator tells faculty members that their department will be permitted to recruit a strong researcher, that action is appreciated by the faculty, for the presence of an active scholar brings attention to the department and indirectly enhances every member's reputation.

On the other hand, administrators do not gain popularity by urging a department to recruit a first-rate teacher, for such an individual can actually irritate colleagues. How many faculty members are comfortable admitting that a colleague's class size is larger because of that individual's superior teaching skills? Or that another faculty member has far more visitors during office hours because the instructor relates better to students? In such a situation the inclination is to chalk up a colleague's success to mere popularity.

Indeed, in an effort to prevent too many students from registering for a course with a favorite instructor, a department, supported by the administration and against the wishes of the teacher, may place an arbitrary limit on class size and hope thereby to maintain the absurd fiction that all its members are equally skilled in the classroom. When such a policy is in place, students who have paid many thousands of dollars to attend that college may be blocked from taking a desired course because a large enrollment would deflate the egos of other professors.

While the judgment of faculty members about their own scholarly accomplishments is usually accurate, their self-assessment of pedagogical skills is often overblown. Indeed, a study has demonstrated that over 90 percent of faculty members believe their teaching performance is above average.[1] The administration does not wish to puncture that balloon and thereby rile the faculty, whose support contributes to an administrator's success. Thus whatever happens in classrooms is treated as not subject to review.

Hence, if an unhappy student complains to a dean about an inadequate teacher, what is the likely response? A shrug of the shoulders and a look that says, "What can I do about it?" So much for the administration's commitment to teaching.

8

Choosing Administrators

Such disappointment with the performance of many administrators raises the question of how they are chosen. Perhaps surprisingly, the steps for selecting provosts and deans are remarkably similar from school to school. A search committee is formed, usually consisting of faculty, students, and other administrators. Then an advertisement is placed, a hundred or so applications are received, the list is shortened, letters of reference are obtained, another cut is made, campus interviews are conducted, recommendations are presented, and the final decision is made by the occupant of the next-highest rung on the administrative ladder.

The process is invariably exhausting, yet the results are often disappointing. The candidate who appears confident and genial during interviews may turn out in office to be ineffective, evasive, or irresponsible. The rejected candidate whose crusty manner or candid opinions put off some committee members may be offered an administrative position elsewhere and become widely admired for trustworthiness, conscientiousness, and acumen.

Mistakes are, of course, inevitable, but judgments at least should be made on the basis of the best available evidence. Yet committees all too often proceed on the mistaken assumption that the most important information about a candidate is to be found in a curriculum vitae, letters from a candidate's supporters, and observations of a candidate's demeanor in a series of brief meetings during a campus visit.

What is missing? The most reliable indication of future performance is past performance, and the quality of past performance is not found in a vita, a supporter's letter, or a brief question-and-answer session. The vita lists the positions held, not the quality of performance in each position, while interviews tell more about the candidate's surface personality and oral facility than sagacity or dependability. As for letters of recommendation, they are notoriously unhelpful. Even Stalin could have obtained glowing letters from three of his colleagues, attesting to his consultative management style, creative leadership, and sense of humor.

The best evidence is to be found not in what a candidate's friends say but in the judgments attested to by a variety of individuals who hold responsible positions at the candidate's campus. What does the chair of the senate say about the candidate's commitment to upholding the appropriate authority of the faculty? What does the chair of the curriculum committee report about the candidate's attitude toward rethinking requirements? What does the chair of the appointments committee tell about the candidate's standards for appointments and promotions, and whether those decisions are impacted by concerns about quality of teaching? What do departmental chairs relate about the candidate's approach to making budgetary decisions? Do the chairs find the candidate accessible, resourceful, fair-minded, and committed to enhancing academic quality? Do other administrators or administrative assistants view the candidate as thoughtful or impulsive, patient or irritable, collegial or overbearing, forgiving or vindictive?

During an interview of a few hours, a candidate may appear good-natured and high-minded, but those who have long observed the individual's character, including at times of personal confrontation or moments of institutional crisis, are beyond being fooled. Yet how to avoid being misled by first impressions?

A search committee should inform each finalist that at least one member or, better yet, several members of the committee will be calling or, preferably, visiting members of the candidate's academic community. While a request can be honored that a particular person, thought to be negatively biased, not be contacted, a candidate who objects to the whole procedure should be passed over. After all, the individual's desire to retain confidentiality is outweighed by the committee's obligation to make the soundest possible decision.

If the information thus obtained suggests that the administrator's performance was less than first-rate, the committee may reasonably assume the person will do no better at the next position. An administrator who micromanaged at one campus is a good bet to try to do so at the next. Someone who wasted money at one institution is unlikely to spend wisely at another. During interviews, a candidate may give the impression of welcoming constructive criticism, but if numerous colleagues who have worked with the person report to the contrary, their testimony should be considered decisive.

Indeed, were I forced to rely either on a vita, letters of recommendation, and interviews or solely on the judgments of numerous previous colleagues, I would select the latter. Search committees, however, do not face this forced option. They can continue to consider the usual information while supplementing it with the best available evidence. Such a procedure would lead to greater satisfaction with the performance of those entrusted with administrative responsibilities.

As to the faculty's view of the search process, I recall a meeting of department chairs during a search for a dean where one faculty member warned the group that the administration was seeking to appoint someone they could control. To which another participant responded, "And what are *we* looking for?"

The obvious answer to that rhetorical question was, "Someone *we* can control." But first-rate deans are not controlled by anyone. Like all effective leaders, they are principled yet practical. They understand how to move the faculty toward worthy goals without arousing unnecessary antagonism. Yet the task is daunting, and goodwill can rapidly dissipate.

This phenomenon is captured in the oft-told tale of the retiring dean who informed a successor of three letters the former left in the desk to aid the latter in times of trouble. When a crisis arose, the new dean opened the first letter and read, "Blame the old dean." The maneuver succeeded, and the problem passed. When another arose, the dean opened the second letter and read, "Blame the old dean." Again the strategy worked. But a further predicament developed, and the dean optimistically hurried to open the third letter. It read, "Prepare three letters."

Faculty members rarely have affection for any administrator. After all, the faculty member's highest priority is the welfare of the department, whereas the administrator's highest priority is the welfare of the entire school, and these two goals may conflict.

In such a situation, the worthy administrator may be required to decline even a sensible departmental request, but how to do so without arousing antagonism? Few can pass that test year after year. As a result, administrators change jobs frequently.

9

Curricular Structure

While students at medical school are required to learn anatomy, and students at law school must learn contracts, what should students pursuing a liberal arts degree be required to learn? The question may appear simple, but when posed by a responsible administrator urging the faculty to take appropriate action, the issue is likely to lead to a clash between departmental and institutional concerns.

No one doubts that within departmental majors, requirements are appropriate. I have yet to hear anyone argue that mathematics majors should not have to learn calculus or that music majors should not have to learn harmony. After all, no student is forced to specialize in any field, but once that choice is made, the essentials of the subject need to be mastered. That much is uncontroversial.

But if a student chooses to pursue a liberal arts degree, one that is supposed to provide a basic, systematic understanding of our world, should any subject matter or skills be required?

Administrators at most schools are inclined to answer affirmatively. They seek a curriculum that is educationally justifiable and easily explainable. While a few schools, such as Brown University, have made their selling point the freedom of students to create their own course of study, most administrators are uncomfortable admitting that they award BA degrees to those who have never encountered materials from one or more of the major fields of inquiry, including mathematics and the natural sciences, the social sciences, history and literature, philosophy and logic, or art and music. If every student who graduated from a college possessed knowledge of these subjects, the case for attending and supporting the school would not be hard to defend.

Faculty members, however, recognize that instituting any requirement forces students to take courses in which they may have little or no interest, and teaching reluctant students is especially demanding. On the other hand, working with students who have enrolled of their own accord is far more inviting.

The difficulty with this convenient line of argument is that students may not choose their courses wisely and therefore may construct a program that is either one-sided or muddled. Many faculty members are aware of this situation but believe that if students select foolishly, the problem is theirs, for as adults they have to make their own judgments.

The crux of the issue, however, is that the faculty, not the students, award a diploma, which states that its holder has satisfactorily completed an appropriate course of study and consequently has been awarded a degree. Who declares that individuals have earned this honor? Do they sign their own diplomas? If so, the diplomas would be worthless. Instead, they are granted on the authority of the faculty and therefore are recognized outside the college. Thus the faculty is responsible for guaranteeing that students awarded degrees have acquired relevant knowledge and skills.

To view the matter from a different perspective, consider a physician asked to sign a document attesting to your good health. Suppose you say to the doctor, "Don't bother with my heart. I'll take responsibility for it." Any physician worthy of the name will reply that if you want the doctor's signature, then the doctor decides how the examination should be conducted.

In the face of this reasoning, faculty members are tempted to avoid requirements by instituting an advisory system. Brown University, for example, states that "all students are matched with faculty and peer advisors who provide counsel on important academic decisions."[1]

Leaving aside the oddity of paying tuition to receive advice from another student (even one given the high-flown title of "peer advisor"), consider the following familiar scenario. A student wishes to register only for courses in literature. An adviser urges the student to take classes in other areas, but the student balks. What to do? Different advisory systems offer different solutions.

Suppose students are permitted to disregard the recommendations of their adviser. Then the faculty will be committed to the irresponsible action of awarding degrees to students who may not have acquired the essentials of a liberal education.

Imagine, however, that students are forced to adhere to rules imposed by a so-called adviser. Would students be subject to the same ruling if they were to switch advisers? If different advisers are empowered to impose different rules, then the system is unfair, because one student might be forced to study a laboratory science while another might be permitted to substitute a course in science fiction.

If, however, the rules are uniform across the school, so that changing advisers is pointless, the result is, in effect, to abandon the advisory system and replace it with a set of requirements.

Although many faculty members are reluctant to think about requirements, preferring to concentrate their attention on their own research, most would agree on the nature of a liberal education. But why is it important, and what steps should be taken to ensure that students receive it? Here are important matters about which faculty members may disagree and which hence call for extended consideration.

10

The Case for Liberal Education

Some defenders of liberal education argue that it is the study of subjects of intrinsic rather than instrumental value, learned for their own sake, not as a means to further ends. To cite one proponent of this view, liberal education is "beyond utility."[1] Those who embrace this position are likely to speak longingly of the trivium and quadrivium (the subjects in a medieval education), while expressing far less concern about recent developments in the physical and social sciences. In their eyes the curriculum is a museum for the wisdom of the past, preserved so as to avoid contamination from the laboratory or the marketplace. In the words of Eva T. H. Brann, the instructor at St. John's College whom I just quoted, "Our time is not an era in which the scene of learning can teem with much newness. I believe that possibility began to vanish three centuries ago."[2]

Even those who do not share such antiquarianism may believe that the content of a liberal education is self-justifying. The fundamental flaw in this approach, however, was exposed long ago by John Dewey. Consider these comparatively neglected passages from his *Democracy and Education*: "We cannot establish a hierarchy of values among studies. In so far as any study . . . marks a characteristic enrichment of life, its worth is intrinsic."[3] Hence, "Those responsible for planning and teaching the course of study should have grounds for thinking that the studies and topics included furnish both direct increments to the enriching of lives of the pupils and also materials which they can put to use in other concerns of direct interest."[4] In other words, to argue that the content of liberal education is of intrinsic value and hence self-justifying provides no defense against the counterclaim that some alternative curriculum is also of intrinsic value and therefore also self-justifying.

Another common defense of liberal education appeals to such notions as self-fulfillment, self-cultivation, and self-realization. The suggestion is that these personal goals are most effectively achieved by study of the liberal arts.

This approach, though, faces serious difficulties. No matter how such terms are understood, Garry Kasparov achieved them by playing chess and Diana Taurasi by playing basketball. Yet neither of these activities is central to anyone's concept of a liberal education. On the other hand, a significant number of those who complete such an education are discontented, disaffected, or even disoriented.

A more promising defense emphasizes the usefulness of acquiring a basic understanding of our world. After all, studying the sciences, social sciences, and humanities helps us make sense of the human condition.

A difficulty with this line of argument, however, is that it fails to demonstrate why a liberal education is significant for the many who may lack the fervor to embark on a four-year quest for knowledge. Can the enormous amount of time and money that our society commits to education be justified as a glorious effort to enable millions to sip from the font of wisdom? In that case, prudence might dictate that in light of our society's limited resources, we ought to provide a liberal education only to potential intellectuals, while furnishing all others with job training. Even if that policy is rejected as inconsistent with our country's commitment to equality of opportunity, the crucial issue is why a specialist needs a general education. For example, why should a future lawyer be required to study music, a future musician chemistry, or a future chemist the foundations of law?

Some proponents of liberal education respond by observing that the most useful preparation for any career is not job training. They argue that the concept of vocational education should be broadened to include scientific, historical, and ethical questions that illuminate any occupational path.

This reply is partially effective but does not demonstrate why an individual ought to study all the essentials of a liberal education. Granted, a future musician might be well advised to study French, German, or Italian; the philosophy of art; and even that branch of physics dealing with acoustics. But why chemistry or biology? Indeed, why any subject whose connection to music is remote?

The four previous justifications mistakenly rest the case for a uniform curriculum on factors differing from person to person. I suggest, instead, that we concentrate on our commonalities—in particular, our mutual responsibilities as free persons in a free society. After all, each of us is not only, for example, a farmer, an electrician, or a nurse but also a citizen, and the welfare of a democracy depends in great part on the understanding and capability of its citizenry. The justification for as many persons as possible to receive a liberal education is that it provides the knowledge, skills, and values all of us need to make a success of our experiment in self-government.

What are these essentials? Here consensus is not hard to reach.

In addition to possessing an understanding of the democratic system itself, every member of a democracy should be able to read, write, and speak effectively so as to be able to participate fully in the free exchange of ideas that is vital to an open society. Every member of a democracy should also be able to comprehend the range of public issues, from poverty, climate change, and ideological conflict, to the dangers of nuclear warfare and the benefits of space research. These topics cannot be intelligently discussed by those ignorant of the physical structure of the world, the forces that shape society, or the ideas and events that form the background of present crises. Thus every member of a democracy should possess substantial knowledge of physical science, social science, world history, and national history.

The study of science assumes familiarity with the fundamental concepts and techniques of mathematics, because such notions play a critical role in the physical sciences and an ever-increasing role in the social sciences. Furthermore, to know only the results of scientific and historical investigations is not sufficient; one needs also to understand the methods of inquiry that have produced these results. No amount of knowledge brings intellectual sophistication unless one also possesses the power of critical thinking. Every member of a democracy, therefore, should be familiar with the canons of logic and scientific method.

Still another characteristic that should be common to all members of a democracy is sensitivity to aesthetic experience. An appreciation of literature, art, and music enriches the imagination, refines the sensibilities, and provides increased awareness of our world. In a society of aesthetic illiterates, not only the quality of art suffers but also the quality of life.

In connection with literature, note that significant value is derived from reading a foreign literature in its original language. Not only does great literature lose some of its richness in translation, but learning another language increases linguistic sensitivity and makes one more conscious of the unique potentialities and limitations of any particular tongue.

Such study is also a most effective means of widening cultural horizons, for understanding another language is a key to understanding another culture.

Every member of a democracy should also acquire intellectual perspective, the ability to scrutinize the fundamental principles of thought and action, encompassing both what is and what ought to be. The path to such wisdom lies in the study of those subtle analyses and grand visions that compose philosophy. No other subject affords a stronger defense against intimidation by dogmatism while simultaneously providing a framework for the operation of intelligence.

Thus we arrive at a justification for the study of liberal education. The more who undertake it, the better, for the ignorance of some is a threat to all. If anyone complains that our democracy provides too much education for too many, they reveal their misunderstanding of a democratic society, for how can the electorate be too educated, know too much, or be too astute? Too little education, however, and democracy may disappear.

But given that this account of the fundamentals of a liberal education is noncontroversial, why is the instituting of appropriate requirements so problematic? The answer, as we shall see, reveals much about how professors think.

11

Requirements

Agreement on ends does not imply accord on means. Thus even faculty members who agree on the importance of liberal education may be reluctant to take responsibility for ensuring that students acquire it.

For example, while I was chairing the Philosophy Department at the University of Vermont, the college undertook a search for a new dean of arts and sciences. When the finalists came to campus, department heads were invited to interview them, and I decided to ask every candidate the same two questions. My first was, "Should our graduates have a basic understanding of the physical structure of the world?" Each candidate agreed confidently that they should. Then I continued: "Can I therefore assume that you favor a science requirement for the bachelor's degree?" Almost all candidates suddenly faltered, seeking some way to reconcile their support for the study of science with their worries about requiring it. Only one candidate, chemist John G. Jewett, responded directly: "I *do* favor a science requirement, plus a mathematics requirement."

Later, at an informal reception, one of my colleagues approached Jewett and expressed concern about his answer.

"I'm unsure about your idea to increase requirements. Don't you think we should proceed cautiously?"

"Why?" asked Jewett. "Do you have another plan?"

"No," said my colleague.

"Then why not try mine?"

I was pleased when Jewett was appointed, and decades later the college still has a requirement that graduates study both mathematics and science. (Incidentally, I once heard Jewett described as "the scourge of those who despise merit.")

Instituting requirements, however, is invariably a struggle. Regardless of how strongly the administration may favor them, the faculty decide what to do and bear the burden of implementing any plan. Hence the needed consensus is always elusive.

Indeed, any faculty meeting that considers requirements is inevitably raucous, and the pattern of debate is all too predictable. First, the head of the school's curriculum committee introduces a motion to the effect that all students be required to study a laboratory science, a foreign language, or perhaps the history of Western civilization. Regardless of the specific content of the motion, one sincere soul soon takes the floor to deliver a rambling speech that concludes resignedly with the rhetorical question, "But why should we place such restrictions on our students?"

The meeting then turns into chaos as the original motion is buried under an avalanche of amendments to the motion, substitute motions, and amendments to the substitute motions. Hours later, when exhaustion sets in, a survivor of the marathon session moves to table the entire matter. Amid sighs of relief, this motion passes (thankfully it is undebatable), the meeting is adjourned, faculty members stagger out of the auditorium, and on each succeeding graduation day students receive their diplomas without having had to demonstrate any knowledge of a laboratory science, a foreign language, or the history of Western civilization.

Several factors contribute to deadlock. To begin, professors are specialists, and for most the central concern is their own field, not anyone else's. This point was emphasized for me at a meeting of the heads of graduate programs at the City University of New York, when an administrator was discussing the difficulties faced by the Biology program and asked whether anyone had ideas for solving the problem. The head of the English program raised his hand and said, "I don't know what to suggest, but I have to say candidly that I don't really care about Biology. If it collapses, so be it. My only concern is English."

Given that such an attitude is widespread among faculty members, why would they want to institute requirements that would force their students to study subjects about which the faculty themselves are unconcerned? In fact, some of the faculty may have studied those subjects in school and done poorly.

A college friend of mine who excelled in all his courses once said to me, "People are as proud of their intellectual weaknesses as of their strengths." Think, for example, how often you have heard someone say with pride, "I can't do math," or, "I'm not a scientist." A faculty member may have a profound knowledge of the Victorian novel yet long ago have given up trying to learn mathematics or science. Why, then, would such a professor favor a requirement in those areas? Analogously, some faculty members have virtually no knowledge of classical music. Why would they support a rule that all students, in order to receive a college degree, need to study Bach, Beethoven, Brahms, and Bartok?

One other factor may be the most important. How much support departments receive from the administration depends on student enrollments. As class sizes rise, the department's case for a new appointment is strengthened; if the numbers decline, the department may not be permitted to fill a vacancy. Thus an issue on everyone's mind is how any proposed requirement would affect each department's enrollment. For example, if a foreign-language requirement is instituted, more students have to enroll in foreign-language courses, thus affecting other departments negatively. Only if a change in requirements is seen as neutral or favorable to a department would its members be willing to consider the proposal.

As a result, trading requirements is a common practice. If I support a science requirement, will you support a history requirement? Therefore the details of a successful curricular plan are likely to include anomalies that result not from fundamental principles but from departmental self-interest. Thus does academic politics affect educational policies.

12

Distribution Requirements

The most obvious way to gain faculty support for ensuring that students bring some semblance of balance to their choice of classes is to divide the curriculum into areas, then require a certain number of courses in each. Because this system favors no department and requires no faculty members to devote their time to developing new offerings, this plan is the easiest to pass. It is referred to as a distribution requirement and is the most common curricular structure in American colleges.

Consider, for example, Williams College, an eminent liberal arts school where the so-called divisional requirement classifies courses into three areas: language and the arts, social studies, and science and mathematics.[1] Language and the arts include art history, art studio, classics, comparative literature, dance, English, foreign languages, music, and theater. Social studies include anthropology, cognitive science, economics, history, philosophy, political science, psychology, religion, and sociology. Science and mathematics include astronomy, biology, chemistry, computer science, maritime studies, mathematics, neuroscience, physics, and statistics. Students must complete at least three courses from each area, thereby obtaining some breadth.

The difficulties with this approach, however, are obvious. Because students have innumerable courses in each division from which to choose, the result may still be a remarkably narrow education. For instance, a student could fulfill the language and the arts requirement by taking Drawing, Photography, and Costume Design, then graduating with a liberal arts degree without having studied English literature or a foreign language. Similarly, a student could fulfill the social studies requirement by taking the New Testament, Earliest Christianities, and the Development of Christianity, then graduating without having studied economics, political science, sociology, or religions other than Christianity. Analogously, a student could fulfill the science and mathematics requirement by taking only courses in statistics and none in science.

In addition, the areas themselves are somewhat arbitrary. After all, is a course in philosophy of art not allied to the study of art? And is symbolic logic not allied with mathematics? Yet both subjects are classified under philosophy, which is filed under social studies. Furthermore, why can students graduate without a course in history or philosophy but not without a course in language or the arts? Perhaps academic politics was originally involved, but few may remember.

In any case, the advantages of such a curriculum redound to faculty members, who can assure themselves that each student has taken courses across the curriculum, while professors teach the same courses they would have offered even if no requirements were in place. In addition, no department stands to gain or lose enrollment from the requirement. As a result, the administration can announce a structured curriculum, students can take virtually whatever they want, and the faculty can focus on their specializations.

All may appear in order, except that a student may be awarded a degree with no knowledge beyond the high school level in literature, history, science, foreign languages, music, or art, and may have no notion of issues in economics, political science, sociology, or philosophy. To quote the British philosopher J. L. Austin, writing in another context, "These seem to be rather serious deficiencies."[2]

To avoid them, why not increase the number of areas, then restrict the courses in each that fulfill the requirement? Thus treat language and the arts as two areas, not one, and require courses in both literature and arts. Then restrict the acceptable courses to those that offer appropriate depth and breadth. For example, Introduction to Comparative Literature would count; Hollywood Films would not. The latter is an appropriate subject for study, but given that students may take only one course in the area of literature, I doubt that most English professors would urge students to study movies rather than Homer, Shakespeare, George Eliot, or James Joyce.

The most extreme version of a distribution requirement would be for the areas to be numerous and the courses to be limited, even to the extent of one course per area. In such a case the pressures on the faculty to offer the required courses would be considerable, and only an especially dedicated group would undertake such a program. Nowadays such an approach is rarely, if ever, found, but I am familiar with at least one historical precedent.

When I came to New York University, I found a curriculum that today would strike faculty and students as astounding. A major figure in the implementation of this remarkable course of study was philosopher Sidney Hook, who was joined by a cadre of extraordinary scholar-teachers, including mathematician Morris Kline, physicist Morris Shamos, political scientist Rita Cooley, and many others who were all determined to present their subjects so as to be accessible to all students.

Here, in their own words, is the curriculum they developed in the 1950s for what was called the Unified Studies Division of Washington Square College of Liberal Arts and Sciences. All students spent their first two years fulfilling these requirements, then pursued a conventional major.

Competent writing and reading are essential to all other studies and for most occupations in later life; therefore, a basic course in English fundamentals is given in the freshman year. This course is followed by one in the literature of Western Europe, introducing the students to their literary heritage. European culture is explored further in a one-term course in the history and literature of Greece and Rome.

A full-year history course then surveys the major developments—political, social, economic, and cultural— that mark the changing fortunes of European civilization from the decline of Rome to the present. A one-term course in philosophical analysis acquaints the students with the great philosophical systems in Western culture and introduces them to the techniques of philosophical thinking.

Because of the interest in the arts and because of their place in the development of civilization, students take a year-long course in the history of either music or art.

International communication in all fields of knowledge, as well as in political and business relations, has become increasingly important and urgent. In consequence, the College requires that before graduation every student should have a reasonable command of one foreign language.

Four one-term courses in the social sciences introduce the student to sociology, the picture of the social structure in which we live; psychology, the study of human experience and behavior; government, the theory, operation, and politics of the American political system compared with other systems; and economics, the study of how people make a living.

Science and mathematics are essential parts of a modern liberal arts education; the basic values inherent in both go far beyond the practical significance attained by them in modern times. The science segment of the program is designed to give the student these values without, however, inserting the detail needed by the specialist. The sequence begins with a one-term course in mathematics, followed by a term of physical science. The student then pursues a one-term laboratory course in either biology, chemistry, geology, or physics.[3]

In the late 1960s, this curriculum, like so many others of the time, was destroyed, then replaced by a weak distribution requirement. Although not many schools ever offered such an exemplary program as that developed at NYU, today's faculty members would be surprised if they went to their school library and found a catalog from the 1950s. Invariably, the curriculum described there demanded far more of both students and faculty than the school's current version.

In fact, in the early 1970s, while at NYU teaching a large course in philosophy of education, I experimented by announcing in class that some faculty members had urged instituting a new curriculum. Without revealing the source, I described the NYU plan from five years before. My students were aghast and complained that no one could handle so much material. Then I revealed that although this approach was not likely to be instituted, it was the exact one completed by their older brothers and sisters who had been graduated recently from NYU. Much had been asked from them, and they met those expectations. Lowering aspirations, however, is likely to produce less accomplishment.

13

A Core Curriculum

Distribution requirements, whether lax or demanding, rely for the most part on courses chosen from departmental offerings. But these, by their very nature, reflect a single discipline.

Suppose a faculty develops a multidisciplinary plan that calls on instructors from various fields to pool their efforts and provide all beginning students, before their choice of major, with the same foundation for a liberal education. That plan is known as a core curriculum, and nowadays it is a rarity.

A long-standing, exemplary one is offered at my alma mater, Columbia College, the relatively small, coeducational liberal arts college within Columbia University. Even though the essentials of the college's program date back to the first half of the twentieth century, they are not widely known. Yet the model is so remarkable that I want to outline it, hoping that doing so may be helpful in suggesting curricular options.[1]

While undergraduates at Columbia may choose from more than eighty majors, over forty concentrations, and hundreds of electives, all students are required to take not only a one-semester course in expository writing, four semesters of a foreign language, two semesters of science, and two semesters from the global core but also the following five courses:

Introduction to Contemporary Civilization in the West
    (two semesters)
Masterpieces of Western Literature and Philosophy
    (two semesters)
Masterpieces of Western Art (one semester)
Masterpieces of Western Music (one semester)
Frontiers of Science (one semester)

The oldest part of the core is *Contemporary Civilization*, developed in 1919 to inquire into issues of war and peace. In the school's words, the course aims "to introduce students to a range of issues concerning the kind of communities—political, social, moral, and religious—that human beings construct for themselves and the values that inform and define such communities; the course is intended to prepare students to become active and informed citizens."[2]

While the reading list has changed over time, here is a recent one:

FIRST SEMESTER

Plato, *Republic* (entire)
Aristotle, *Nicomachean Ethics* and *Politics*
Hebrew Bible, *Exodus* 1–24; *Deuteronomy* 1–6; *I Samuel* 8–10,
    17–20; *Ecclesiastes* (entire)
New Testament, *Matthew* 3–7; *Romans* (entire); *Galatians*
    (entire)
Augustine, *City of God*
Qur'an
Medieval Philosophy (selections by Ibn Tufayl, Al-Ghazali,
    and Thomas Aquinas)
Machiavelli, *The Prince*

New World (selections by Sepulveda and Vitoria)
Protestant Reformation (selections edited by Hans
    Hillerbrand)
Scientific Revolution (selections by Descartes)
Hobbes, *Leviathan*
Locke, *Second Treatise*

SECOND SEMESTER

Rousseau, *Discourse on Inequality* and *Social Contract*
Smith, *Treatise on Moral Sentiments*
Kant, *Groundwork of the Metaphysics of Morals*
Smith, *Wealth of Nations*
Burke, *Reflections on the Revolution in France*
Wollstonecraft, *A Vindication of the Rights of Woman*
Tocqueville, *Democracy in America*
Mill, *On Liberty*
Mill and Taylor, *The Subjection of Women*
Elizabeth Cady Stanton, "Address to the Legislature of
    New York"
Sojourner Truth, "Ain't I a Woman?"
Marx, selection from the *Marx-Engels Reader*
Darwin, *Origin of Species* and *Descent of Man*
Nietzsche, *On the Genealogy of Morals*
Du Bois, *The Souls of Black Folk* and "Souls of White Folk"
Freud, selections from the *Freud Reader*
Gandhi, "Swaraj" (On self-rule)
Fanon, "On Violence," in *The Wretched of the Earth*
Foucault, *Discipline and Punish*

The course is taught in sections of twenty to twenty-five students and requires faculty members from different departments to cooperate in the planning. The result differs from any single department's offerings.

The same is true of *Literature Humanities*, which dates back to 1937. In the school's words, it "is designed to enhance students' understanding of main lines of literary and philosophical development that have shaped western thought for nearly three millennia. Much more than a survey of great books, Lit Hum encourages students to become critical readers of the literary past we have inherited. Although most of our Lit Hum works (and the cultures they represent) are remote from us, we nonetheless learn something about ourselves in struggling to appreciate and understand them."[3] Again, the course is taught in small sections with instructors from a range of departments.

Here is a recent reading list. All works are read in their entirety, except as noted.

FIRST SEMESTER

Homer, *Iliad*

Sappho, *Lyrics*

Homer, *Odyssey*

Hebrew Bible, *Genesis*

Herodotus, *The Histories* (selections)

Aeschylus, *Oresteia*

Euripides, *Bacchae*

Thucydides, *History of the Peloponnesian War* (selections)

Plato, *Symposium*

Virgil, *Aeneid*

Ovid, *Heroides* (selection)

SECOND SEMESTER

New Testament, *Luke* and *John*

Augustine, *Confessions*

Dante, *Inferno*

Boccaccio, *Decameron* (selections)

Montaigne, *Essays*: "To the Reader"; "On Idleness"; "On the Power of the Imagination"; "On Cannibals"; "On Repentance"; and "On Experience"

Shakespeare, *King Lear*

Cervantes, *Don Quixote* (selections)

Milton, *Paradise Lost*

Austen, *Pride and Prejudice*

Dostoevsky, *Crime and Punishment*

Woolf, *To the Lighthouse*

Morrison, *Song of Solomon*

Faculty members who teach this course go beyond their field of specialization, and students, regardless of their future majors, build a foundation for further reading.

A skeptic might wonder what an undergraduate student learns from studying a work such as the *Inferno*. The best answer I ever heard was given years ago at a public event where the core curriculum was being celebrated. An instructor told of a student's coming into her office to complain, "I'm not getting anything out of Dante." To which she replied, "The issue is not what you're getting out of Dante; the issue is what Dante is getting out of you." Or, as the college writes, "Lit Hum encourages us to compare our own assumptions and values to the radically different ones expressed in our readings. It demands that we examine ourselves in relation to our past." In short, if the student was not led to self-reflection by reading Dante, the fault lay not with Dante but with the student. (I still recall that in Dante's monumental vision, the greatest sin was treachery to benefactors, and the greatest sinners, held in the three mouths of Lucifer at the bottom of hell, were Brutus, Cassius, and Judas Iscariot.)

Moving from the ugly to the beautiful, I would emphasize that the Columbia core is rare, perhaps unique, in requiring the study of both art and music. If students are given a choice, they almost invariably pick the area they know best, whereas they would surely learn more by enrolling in the other. Columbia, however, does not offer the option.

Art Humanities became part of the core in 1947. In the school's own description, it "is not a historical survey, but an analytical study of a limited number of monuments and artists, and teaches students how to look at, think about, and engage in critical discussion of the visual arts."[4] A typical semester explores in detail the Parthenon, Amiens Cathedral, and the work of Raphael, Michelangelo, Pieter Bruegel, Gian Lorenzo Bernini, Rembrandt van Rijn, Francisco Goya y Lucientes, Claude Monet, Pablo Picasso, Frank Lloyd Wright, Le Corbusier, Jackson Pollock, and Andy Warhol. The course also makes extensive use of New York City through field trips to museums, buildings, and monuments.

Music Humanities, also introduced in 1947, in the college's words, "has awakened in students an appreciation of music in the Western world, it has helped them respond intelligently to a variety of musical idioms, and it has engaged them in the debates about the character and purposes of music that have occupied composers and musical thinkers since ancient times."[5]

The general outline is as follows:

Medieval and Renaissance Music
 Gregorian chant
 Hildegard of Bingen
 Josquin des Prez
 the madrigal
Baroque Music
 Monteverdi

Handel: *Messiah*
Bach: the Brandenburg Concertos
Classical Music
    Haydn: instrumental works
    Mozart: operas and instrumental works
    Beethoven: symphonies
Romantic Music
    Schubert (the Lied)
    Chopin
    Berlioz: *Symphonie fantastique*
    Wagner
    Verdi
Twentieth-Century Music
    Debussy
    Stravinsky: *The Rite of Spring*
    Berg: *Wozzeck*
    Schonberg
American Composers
    Ives
    Copland
    Cage
Jazz
    Armstrong
    Ellington
    Parker

Like Art Humanities, Music Humanities is taught in small sections and takes advantage of cultural life in New York City. Attending a concert or opera may be routine to some students, but for many others the course takes them to places they never would have gone and offers them experiences they never would have enjoyed. Not surprisingly, as a result of having taken this course, many Columbia students develop a lifetime devotion to music.

One advantage of requiring the art and music courses is that students do not face the intimidating prospect of learning either subject surrounded by those already passionate about it. Here most are beginners, and the course is structured with them in mind.

Frontiers of Science was added to the core in 2004. As the course is described, "it is designed to instill skills more generally characteristic of the scientific approach to inquiry, in the context of several scientific disciplines." A recent semester's subjects included "elements of neuroscience, astrophysics, Earth science, and biodiversity. . . . The first two put larger questions of reality, our place in the Universe, and who we are as humans into scientific context. The Earth science and biodiversity modules connect to important societal issues."[6] *Frontiers of Science* combines a one-day-a-week lecture by a researcher with weekly seminars "to discuss the lecture and associated readings, to undertake in-class activities, and to debate the implications of the most recent scientific discoveries."[7] Like the other core courses, *Frontiers of Science* calls on faculty from different departments to teach across disciplinary boundaries.

Note that the primary beneficiaries of a core curriculum are the students, not the faculty. No wonder, then, that the strongest supporters of the Columbia core are the alumni, who recognize the value of having been provided with a breadth of vision that illuminates any subsequent specialization.

Granted, other schools make a virtue of encouraging students to follow their own interests, wherever they may lead. But these often develop haphazardly, without systematic exploration of available alternatives. What students happen to find interesting at the time they select their courses may be the result of suggestions from relatives or friends, the influences of the media, or the effects of good or bad teaching in elementary and secondary schools. Perhaps a family subscription to *Psychology Today* sparked an interest in that subject, while a roommate's bad experience in a philosophy course discouraged the pursuit of that inquiry. To consider a more pointed example, a monomaniacal premed student may be interested only in the natural sciences, believing work in the social sciences or humanities irrelevant to a physician's responsibilities.

Such cases illustrate that for a freshman to be asked to choose sensibly from thousands of available classes is an unfortunate situation that arises from the faculty's unwillingness to construct and teach courses that provide the fundamentals of a liberal education. How much easier for faculty members to leave matters to the students, even if they are unprepared for that responsibility. They may waste time and money, but meanwhile the professors can continue their research undisturbed.

To see the problem vividly, just show Columbia's Literary Humanities reading list to a professor of literature and ask if studying the works listed is worth a student's time. Almost every faculty member will answer affirmatively. Then ask: Would you be willing to teach a course with this reading list? Almost all will refuse. Therein lies the problem of creating a strong curricular structure.

14

Departments

We have seen the central role departments play in creating a curriculum, and they lie at the heart of academic life. If, in former Speaker of the House Tip O'Neill's words, "all politics is local," then we can say that in academia, "all politics is departmental."

A professor's appointment is not simply to the school's faculty but to a particular department, and each, like a family, is unique. To paraphrase the opening of *Anna Karenina*, all happy departments are alike, but each unhappy department is unhappy in its own fashion.

The ideal is a friendly department where colleagues who might disagree intellectually nevertheless provide mutual support, offer one another pedagogical advice, comment on one another's scholarly papers, and work together for the common good. In such an atmosphere, the welfare of students is treated as of prime importance, and they are able to pursue their studies without the detrimental effects of personal animosities among the faculty.

Yet other departments are filled with discord. In one, authoritarian rule leads to resentment and eventual rebellion, while in another, infirm leadership results in anarchy. Some are beset by hostile factions engaged in a variety of personal, political, or scholarly disputes. Although the origins of such battles may be shrouded in ancient history, the feuds live on and continue to divide the members. In such struggles, students are typically used as pawns, and their academic needs are virtually forgotten.

The departmental cast of characters includes those who stress research, those who focus on teaching, those who perform much school service, and some who excel in two or even all three areas. Unfortunately, we may also find those who are barely adequate in any.

I myself have had as colleagues such memorable figures as a crusty old-timer with few publications who taught the same courses with the same reading lists for decades; a fading scholar whose alcoholism began to overshadow his considerable academic achievements; a successful writer and teacher who became disengaged from departmental responsibilities and left to join the faculty at another school in order to obtain a better pension plan; a prolific scholar who was eventually consumed by debauchery; a sincere but ineffective teacher without scholarly ambition who inherited a fortune and lost interest in academic pursuits; a fine scholar and strong teacher whose work was gradually overtaken by a passion for radical politics; and a beginner who published papers in prestigious journals but found academic life not to his liking and embarked instead on a promising career as a lawyer.

A further complication is that successful members of the same department may approach their common discipline with strikingly different interests and methodologies. I recall an incident involving a celebrated analytic philosopher who entered an elevator in his office building and found himself alone with an equally famous, old-time historian of philosophy. They had never met before, and exchanged not a word until coming to their common floor, then going separate ways. As the analytic philosopher later remarked, "I couldn't think of anything to say to him."

How much does an expert in Chaucer share with another professor of English who specializes in the novels of Faulkner? These two may reside in the same department yet have little in common.

Students often suppose that although they find difficulty in dealing with certain professors, faculty members themselves get along amiably. Nothing could be further from the truth. Departments can be filled with animosities, and professors may be glad they do not have to study with certain colleagues whose work they consider inadequate and whose personalities they find grating.

These tensions come to the fore in departmental meetings. Some might suppose that those whose lives center on reasoned discussion would behave at academic meetings in exemplary fashion. Such is not the case. Actually, remarkably few professors are able to transfer their scholarly skills to discussions of practical issues. Just present the group with a real-life problem, and the meeting is apt to turn into a mélange of reminiscences, irrelevancies, and impracticalities. Rarely can consensus be reached, and even then likely fails to do justice to the complexities of the problem. Once in a while, however, a faculty member demonstrates the ability to think clearly and offer practical solutions. That person is apt to become a departmental chair and, if willing, may be on track to a career in administration.

An academic once remarked that his colleagues possess "cognitive abilities of a special sort, which are . . . extremely sophisticated *relative* to the population norm."[1] I can only suppose he had never witnessed a departmental meeting.

15

Appointments

Whatever discord may permeate a department, when a vacancy appears, all members will urge the dean to allow it to be filled. After all, a larger department is a stronger one, for it enrolls more students and receives a greater share of administrative support. Searching for a new colleague, however, is rarely a smooth process and can intensify departmental friction or create it where none existed.

Once a department is informed that it can make an appointment, the announcement of the position needs to be developed. The question then arises as to which subfields, if any, will be given prominence in the search. Ideally, the decision should reflect fair assessment of the department's needs. Too often, however, that criterion is ignored.

Imagine a music department that has four members teaching the history of Western music. Let us designate them as *A*, *B*, *C*, and *D*. *A* teaches Renaissance music; *B* specializes in the baroque age, particularly J. S. Bach; *C* focuses on the classical period, especially Beethoven; and *D* teaches music of the twentieth and twenty-first centuries. What is missing?

A neutral observer would immediately recognize a crucial gap: composers of the romantic era, including Brahms and Wagner.

That era, however, may *not* be the department's first priority. Consider how the discussion might proceed:

A: I'm supposed to cover all of Renaissance music, but I focus on the early period. We need someone for the late.

B: While my work is centered on Bach, there's so much more in the baroque. Let's add someone who can handle it. The nineteenth century is important, but I haven't heard much call from students for Tchaikovsky.

C: Recently I've been concentrating on Beethoven's quartets. How about someone who can delve into Haydn and Mozart? We can also use someone who could teach the yearlong survey in the history of music.

D: Contemporary music is so varied that we need another person to do it justice. I have a friend from graduate school who works in electronic music and would be a terrific colleague.

The pattern is clear. Every member hopes to use the appointment to advance personal interests.

Here is commentary to help explain the discussion.

A, the historian of the Renaissance, seeks a colleague with similar interests so as to have someone at hand for discussion and assistance. Rather than saying so, however, *A* stresses differences between the early and later Renaissance, then argues that the department needs a specialist in both. The problem, of course, is that any subject can be divided into smaller units and the argument made that each unit needs coverage. We might term this strategy "divide and augment."

Suppose, for instance, instead of one professor doing Shakespeare, we split the field into tragedies, histories, comedies, and romances, then argue for specialists in each area. And how about someone to cover Shakespeare's sonnets? Suddenly five professors are teaching Shakespeare.

In a large department, multiple scholars for a single area might be reasonable, but this small program has room for only one historian of Renaissance music.

B, the historian of baroque music, also uses the "divide and augment" strategy, followed by an appeal to lack of student interest in nineteenth-century music. But why expect students to urge that a subject they have never studied should be taught? If baroque music were not in the curriculum, would students complain?

C, the scholar of the classical period, wants to focus on Beethoven, and also seeks someone to teach the history of music survey that requires extensive preparation and covers materials outside any one instructor's interests. *C* proposes that the members of the department avoid that demanding assignment by giving it to a newcomer.

D, the contemporary music scholar, uses the "divide and augment" strategy, then adds what might be labeled the "I have a friend" approach. This maneuver typically leads a professor to overrate pals, then become angry if colleagues do not share this inflated view. To avoid the problem, all department members should agree that in considering candidates, no one is under any obligation to be favorably disposed toward anyone else's friend. All subsequent discussion of candidates should be untarnished by personal attachments, and anyone suggesting a friend should stay out of discussion of that candidate. Failure to do so is one of the most common reasons for unfortunate appointments.

Once the members of the department present their opinions, the discussion usually turns repetitive and possibly rather unpleasant, as each one reiterates ever more forcefully already-stated positions. In accord with academic manners, however, attacks are never launched against the value of anyone else's research area but instead framed as defenses of one's own. How to break the impasse?

One solution calls for the advertisement to include a list of specializations sought: the late Renaissance, the baroque age, Haydn and Mozart, the nineteenth century, and electronic music. That approach will likely satisfy the four members but appear strange to potential candidates who will wonder why the department has such an unusual collection of priorities.

Here an effective dean might step in and insist that the complex advertisement be sharpened. Such a request, although sensible, is why faculty consider administrators to be obstacles.

How might the department react to the dean's objection? A common move is to declare that the search will seek the best person, regardless of field. This step might temporarily satisfy all involved, but down the road produce poor results.

The reason is revelatory. While specialists have some acquaintance with other subject matters, only regarding their own are they familiar with a broad spectrum of faculty members, programs, and scholarly activities. Therefore, unless one candidate is clearly superior to all others (a rare situation), each professor will find "the best" to be the best in that specialist's field and try to forge a majority in favor of that candidate. As the infighting continues, the field most likely to be neglected is the one currently unrepresented; it is least known by the members, yet most in need of an appointment. In the end, however, whichever professor is politically savvy and most determined carries the day. If, after a year or two, another opening appears and again the same area is disregarded, the department will become lopsided, perhaps for decades.

Why did this situation develop? Because the dean allowed the department to advertise the position as open. What should have happened is that when the compromise was proposed, the dean should have responded, "No one's working in the nineteenth century. Unless that's the specialty you announce, the search is over." The department would be upset but likely bow to the dean in order to make an appointment.

Eventually, if the dean monitors the search process carefully, the department will settle on a candidate who can cover the romantic period. As a result, the students will benefit and have the opportunity to study the music of Mendelssohn, Chopin, and Verdi, among so many other favorites. Even the faculty may eventually appreciate the perspective of their new colleague and realize the wisdom of offering broader coverage.

In any case, discord is likely to accompany the process. Indeed, if for nefarious reasons someone wanted to create turmoil in an amiable department, I cannot think of a more effective strategy than offering the members an opportunity to undertake a search. Even if they do not reach consensus, they should consider themselves fortunate if their good relations survive.

16

Tenure and Academic Freedom

While faculty members may disagree about the structure of the curriculum or the priorities for new appointments, their disputes take place from a standpoint shared by virtually all: belief in the system of tenure, according to which those who possess it hold lifetime appointments, revocable only in rare instances of gross incompetence or moral turpitude. Yet reference to this prerogative invariably gives rise to the same questions: Why should anyone receive permanent job security? And does tenure not pamper the indolent and protect the incompetent?

Academic tenure is not as singular as often supposed. In most organizations of university size, employees, whether at lower ranks or in middle management, are rarely dismissed for cause. As a result of poor performance, they may be passed over for promotion, given lateral transfers, or occasionally demoted, but seldom are they discharged. Just as plant closings or fiscal crises may precipitate worker layoffs, tenured professors, too, face the loss of their positions if a department is phased out or a school closes.

Even the mechanics of the tenure system are hardly unique. Consider large law firms, which routinely recruit new associates with the understanding that after several years they will either be offered some variety of permanent position or required to depart. Colleges make similar arrangements with beginning faculty members.

Despite such analogies, however, tenure undoubtedly provides professors an unusual degree of latitude and security. They are privileged to explore any area of interest, and to proceed in whatever manner they wish. No one may dictate to them that certain subjects are taboo, that certain methods of inquiry are illegitimate, or that certain conclusions are unacceptable.

Tenure thus guarantees academic freedom, the right of all qualified persons to discover, teach, and publish the truth as they see it within their fields of competence. Where academic freedom is secure, students enter classrooms with the assurance that instructors are espousing their own beliefs, not mouthing some orthodoxy they have been programmed to repeat. Likewise, academic freedom guarantees that no ideological test is imposed to determine who will be appointed to the faculty. Competence, not creed, is the criterion.

Although academic freedom is widely seen as valuable, it is threatened whenever anyone seeks to stifle free inquiry in the name of a cause that supposedly demands everyone's unthinking allegiance. Some, for example, have sought to have a school adopt an official stance on issues unrelated to its educational mission. Free inquiry, however, is impeded when certain opinions are officially declared false and others true. Schools are not established to inform the public where a majority of the faculty stands on any issue, whether mathematical, scientific, or political. Whether an argument for the existence of God is sound, or our government's foreign policy misguided, is a matter for discussion, not decree.

Maintaining free inquiry requires that all points of view be entitled to a hearing. Unfortunately, too many both from inside and outside academia have attempted to interfere with a campus speaker's presentation on the grounds that they find the views expressed to be unpalatable. So long as the lecturer remains civil, however, no one at the school, whether professors, students, or administrators, should block any individual from expressing ideas. No matter how noxious they may be, the greater danger lies in stifling them, for when one person's opinion is silenced, no one else's may be uttered in safety.

But might academic freedom be preserved without tenure, perhaps by some form of multiyear contracts? The problem besetting any alternative scheme is that it could too easily be misused, opening faculty members to attack because of their opinions.

A key feature of the tenure system is that those who hold tenure decide whether it should be granted to others. Thus those who judge are not facing a conflict of interest, because their own tenure is not at stake. In any system of multiyear contracts, however, the question arises as to who should decide whether a contract ought to be renewed. If the decision is placed in the hands of other tenured professors, they would be voting while realizing that their own contracts would eventually be up for renewal. The result would be a conflict of interest. After all, if I support your renewal, will you support mine? Worse, the decision might be made by administrators with an ax to grind, favoring contract renewal for professors who have supported administrative initiatives. Such a system would produce an atmosphere of suspicion and recrimination antithetical to independent thinking.

Unquestionably, the tenure system has dangers, but none as great as those that would attend its abandonment. To adapt a remark about democracy offered by Winston Churchill, tenure may be the worst system ever devised, except for all the others.

To defend the tenure system in principle, however, is not to applaud the ways it has been implemented. Without doubt, most colleges and universities have awarded tenure too liberally. Instead of individuals being required to demonstrate why they do deserve tenure, a school has been expected to demonstrate why they do not. In court, a person ought to be presumed not guilty until the evidence shows otherwise, but in matters of special skill, you should not be supposed proficient until so proven. A school's failure to observe this guideline results in a faculty encumbered with deadwood, and more than a few departments suffer from this unfortunate phenomenon.

Yet decisions whether to grant tenure can present difficult problems for both faculty and administrators, and have been known to cause hostilities that last for many years. We have seen how the appointment process can lead to conflict, but it may be a mere skirmish compared to the campus war that can break out over a tenure decision. Yet unpleasant as events may become, faculty members need to act conscientiously, because the future of their schools may be at stake.

To illustrate the problems that can arise, I shall examine in detail one case that caused institutional turmoil. After reading the account, consider how you would have voted, then see whether you concur with my judgment. Regardless, be assured that disagreements in tenure cases are hardly a rarity.

17

A Tenure Case

The following account was authored by the late Paul J. Olscamp, a philosopher who served as president of Western
Washington University (1975–1982), then of Bowling Green
University (1982–1995). So far as I know, the presentation is
factual, but I am not aware of who was involved or where or
when the events occurred.[1]

Dr. Sally Morse (a fictitious name) found herself standing
for tenure and promotion to associate professor. Her
department was targeted by her university as a "niche"
discipline—a discipline or set of disciplines in a single
department that the university wished to develop into a
major player in the state's research environment. Expectations and rewards were higher for this department than
for all others in the university.

Morse submitted her application in her sixth year as a
faculty member. Her teaching evaluations were excellent.
She had few refereed publications, although the ones she
had were in journals of high repute. Morse's service record
was barely adequate, but the department informed the
collegiate-level tenure and promotion committee that this
was because the department discouraged her service
activities and encouraged research in its place.

Morse's research and publication record was clearly good enough to have earned her tenure in almost all of the university departments not designated as "niche." But it was average in comparison to the records of similar applicants from other "niche" programs. In a split vote within her department (6–4 with one abstention), she was recommended for tenure and promotion. Included in her file was a letter from the chair noting that Morse's research protocol was proceeding on schedule, and that the majority of the publications could not be expected until her work was complete. It was also noted that Morse had not attracted significant outside funding from either government or private sources.

On the basis of the department's split vote, the collegiate-level tenure and promotion committee voted 5–4 to deny her tenure and promotion. The committee noted that this decision was particularly difficult for them, because in most other departments her record would have qualified her for tenure and promotion. They also noted the systematic vagueness in the university's standards of excellence with respect to the three evaluative criteria (teaching, research, and service).

The dean of the college recommended that Morse be given tenure but that promotion to associate professor be withheld pending further publication of her research. In his recommendation, the dean noted the split vote of the collegiate committee and their comments on the vagueness of the evaluative criteria. He stated that if "niche" programs were to have higher standards, then the departmental policies should say that and define them.

The university-level tenure and promotion committee overturned the dean's recommendation, agreeing with the collegiate committee, but once again by a split vote, and with the same reservations expressed by the dean.

Olscamp now turns from factual description to an attempted justification of the ultimate decision:

It was clear that the expectations of Morse were much higher than the average for tenure and promotion applicants for the university as a whole. It was also clear that the higher criteria she had to meet were nowhere clearly defined in university policy. Given her record to date, it was reasonably foreseeable that Morse would continue to develop in her research, as well as in other professional categories.

Morse was a superstar teacher, and even in a niche department the school could not afford to lose such a fine instructor without violating its promises to students and their parents.

Olscamp concludes with the outcome:

Dr. Sally Morse was given tenure and promoted. The policies and procedures manuals were and are being revised to correct the deficiencies noted by the committees. The work is still in progress, having proven much more difficult than was anticipated.

The most noticeable feature of this case was Morse's weak support from her colleagues. In the absence of personal animosity, most departmental members are reluctant to deny tenure to colleagues with whom they have worked closely for years. In this case, however, only six out of eleven supported Morse. The college-level tenure and promotion committee voted against tenure, which is uncommon, and the dean clearly had doubts, recommending tenure but not promotion, an unusual procedure because the two usually go together. The university-level tenure and promotion committee also voted against tenure, thereby overturning the dean's recommendation, a rare occurrence.

As for Morse's research, although she was informed at the outset that it should be her first priority, she had few publications and did not attract outside funding, an important criterion for success in most science and some social science departments. That her record was good enough compared to those in other departments is irrelevant, because she had been provided with special support.

As to her teaching, she enjoyed excellent student evaluations, but why did those qualify her as a "superstar" teacher? How many instructors received equally strong evaluations? If she were replaced in the classroom, would quality of instruction be significantly reduced? If not, she could be succeeded by someone who would at least match her as a teacher while surpassing her in scholarly output. Remember that for every opening, hundreds of candidates apply, and retaining her was preventing numerous others from being considered.

In addition, her service was described as "barely adequate," but that failing was excused because she was supposed to focus on research. Yet service can take various forms, many of which are not especially time-consuming, and her failure to find some way to help her colleagues was a mark against her.

Olscamp defends the case for awarding her tenure, but to my mind his arguments fall short. He claims that her research might in the long run yield publications, but who knows? If those being considered for tenure do not publish when the pressure to do so is greatest, why assume they will do so when the strongest incentive has been removed?

He also stresses that criteria for tenure in niche departments were not given with specificity, but he does not say that the situation differed in other departments. In fact, whenever experts assess quality, no simple formula can replace human judgment. Whether an athlete merits selection as an all-star, a pianist deserves a prize at a music competition, or a movie is worthy of an award at a film festival is a decision that goes beyond mere numbers, and the same is the case for granting tenure. No wonder that, as Olscamp relates, the attempt to revise the policies and procedures manual proved much more difficult than anticipated. I doubt the work was ever completed.

The irony of Olscamp's presentation is that Morse was ultimately awarded tenure not because of any scholarly contribution but because of her supposed status as a "superstar" teacher. Her performance in the classroom may have fit that description, and if so, the case for awarding her tenure was strong, but Olscamp offers no evidence beyond excellent student evaluations. Were her colleagues impressed by observing her teaching? Was registration in all her courses unusually strong? If granting tenure depended on her supposedly offering superb instruction, why was more not done to assess it?

In the Morse case, others may arrive at a decision different from mine, particularly by assuming evidence not provided in Olscamp's presentation. The key point, however, is that hard questions need to be asked, and tough decisions may be required. After all, granting tenure is a momentous matter that commits the school to spending millions of dollars in salary and benefits over what is likely to be decades. If a mistake is made, faculty and students will pay the price for generations to come. For that reason, the rule of thumb should be: if in doubt, say no.

In sum, much is at stake whenever any faculty member is awarded or denied tenure. Wise choices are a blessing, foolish ones a blight. Too many ill-advised decisions may bring tenure itself into disrepute, thereby threatening the academic freedom that the system is intended to preserve.

18

Autonomy

In the early 1970s, a book appeared with the provocative title *This Beats Working for a Living: The Dark Secrets of a College Professor.* The author's name was given as Professor X, although I later learned he headed the history department of a state university in the West. His skepticism about faculty members was epitomized in this blunt judgment: "I have met few professors whom I would hire to run a peanut stand, let alone be the guardian of wisdom and Western civilization."[1]

I sympathize with this sentiment yet recall that during my undergraduate years at Columbia College the faculty included such eminent scholars and dedicated teachers as Jacques Barzun, Daniel Bell, Peter Gay, Moses Hadas, Gilbert Highet, Richard Hofstadter, Polykarp Kusch, Meyer Schapiro, and Lionel Trilling, along with others I named earlier. Surely this esteemed group could have been considered, in Professor X's words, "the guardian of wisdom and Western civilization."

None of them, however, believed that a faculty member's responsibilities were limited to research; all were superb teachers and participated heavily in the life of their school.

Yet I recognize that they were exceptions, not the rule. Unfortunately, professors may be dull or lazy, foolish or unethical. But they may also be brilliant and indefatigable, wise and kind. Some are stereotypically absentminded, but others are extraordinarily perceptive. Some were not suited for success elsewhere and retreated to the groves of academia. Others, however, could have had outstanding careers in medicine, law, or business but chose instead the life of a professor.

Such a choice would not have been made on financial grounds but might well have been based on finding joy in teaching and learning, as well as relishing the independence so characteristic of faculty members. After all, few institutions other than colleges and universities permit their members the latitude so much a part of the professor's life.

Tenured professors normally set their own schedules. They teach virtually when they want, what they want, and how they want. They keep whichever office hours they want, attend such faculty meetings as they want, and accept committee assignments to the extent they want.

To appreciate how ingrained such privileges can become, consider a senior professor of my acquaintance who had managed to reduce his schedule to the minimum, appearing in school only on Friday afternoons to teach two graduate seminars separated by one office hour. He had hoped that scheduling classes at that time would minimize the number of students who would enroll. One spring day he was called to his department head's office and asked whether, as a service to students, he might be willing to teach one of his seminars the following fall on Monday afternoons. The suggestion so horrified him that he replied incredulously, "If you don't have Mondays off, what do you have?"

Few attorneys, engineers, or business managers enjoy such options. Indeed, most people, whether in honored professions or low-prestige occupations, are required to be at the workplace from morning until night, assuming tasks they have not specifically chosen, and functioning under the scrutiny of others who assess their performance and to whom they are responsible. This pattern applies equally to vice presidents at General Motors, to their executive assistants, and to workers on their assembly lines.

I am not forgetting those professors who work almost every waking hour, seven days a week, increasing their depth of understanding and adding to their accomplishments. The essential point, however, is that these individuals freely decide their schedule and goals. They do not punch time clocks. They do not conform to organizational demands. Such an extraordinary degree of autonomy can be viewed as an opportunity to help others or an invitation to act selfishly.

Consider the case of one professor who was devoted to exegetical study of the writings of the German philosopher Edmund Husserl (1859–1938), the central figure in the movement known as phenomenology. As a graduate student, this professor took many courses on Husserl and eventually wrote a doctoral dissertation on Husserl, has attended conferences each summer on Husserl, and every semester teaches a course or even two devoted to Husserl. Once, when only two students registered for the Husserl seminar, departmental colleagues asked the professor to offer instead an introductory course that would provide beginners with an understanding of the nature of philosophical inquiry. The professor indignantly refused, insisting that the department should teach only small courses on specialized topics such as Husserl and not be bothered with any students other than its own majors. No one, I hasten to add, had the least success in convincing the professor of the impracticality of this proposal to reform the college curriculum.

Such insularity is unfortunate, typical of the irresponsibility I have witnessed professors exhibit throughout my five decades in academia. Yet I have been equally impressed by those who care deeply about others and take advantage of faculty autonomy to pursue research assiduously, teach attentively, and serve their schools conscientiously.

Inside academia, we find some whose practices are misguided or even shameful, while others act on the highest principles. The former need to be recognized and resisted. The latter deserve to be esteemed and emulated.

Notes

1. How Professors View Academia

1. I take the details of the incident from Rudolph H. Weingart-ner's account in his *A Sixty-Year Ride through the World of Education* (Lanham, Md.: Hamilton Books, 2007), 135.

2. Graduate School

1. Donald H. Naftulin, John E. Ware Jr., and Frank A. Donnelly, "The Doctor Fox Lecture: A Paradigm of Educational Seduction," *Journal of Medical Education* 48 (1973): 630–635. An excerpt from the lecture is available on YouTube.

4. How Teachers Succeed

1. Wilfrid Sellars, "'. . . This I or He or It (the Thing) Which Thinks . . . ,'" *Proceedings and Addresses of the American Philosophical Association* 44 (September 1971): 5.
2. Stuart Hampshire, "A Kind of Materialism," *Proceedings and Addresses of the American Philosophical Association* 43 (September 1970): 5.
3. Victor L. Cahn, *Classroom Virtuoso: Reflections of a Life in Learning* (Lanham, Md.: Rowman and Littlefield, 2009), 5–6.

6. Changing Departmental Culture

1. Charles B. Schultz, "Some Limits to the Validity and Usefulness of Student Rating of Teachers: An Argument for Caution," *Educational Research Quarterly* 3 (1978): 12–27.

7. The Administration

1. Paul C. Price, "Are You as Good a Teacher as You Think?," *Thought and Action*, Fall 2006, 7–14.

9. Curricular Structure

1. "The College," Brown University, accessed June 14, 2018, https://www.brown.edu/academics/college/.

10. The Case for Liberal Education

1. Eva T. H. Brann, *Paradoxes of Education in a Republic* (Chicago: University of Chicago Press, 1979), 62.
2. Brann, 3.
3. John Dewey, *Democracy and Education: The Middle Works of John Dewey, 1899–1924*, ed. Jo Ann Boydston (Carbondale: Southern Illinois University Press, 1980), 9:248
4. Dewey, 250.

12. Distribution Requirements

1. See "Areas of Study," Williams College, accessed June 14, 2018, https://www.williams.edu/academics-p/areas-of-study/.
2. J. L. Austin, *Sense and Sensibilia* (Oxford: Oxford University Press, 1963), 54.
3. New York University, *New York University Bulletin: Washington Square College of Arts and Sciences, 1965–1966* (New York: New

York University, 1965), 30. Minor changes have been made for
the sake of uniformity.

13. A Core Curriculum

1. See "Academic Requirements," Columbia College, accessed
   June 14, 2018, http://bulletin.columbia.edu/columbia-college
   /requirements-degree-bachelor-arts/.
2. "About Contemporary Civilization," Columbia College,
   accessed June 14, 2018, https://www.college.columbia.edu/core
   /classes/cc.php.
3. "About Literature Humanities," Columbia College, accessed
   June 14, 2018, https://www.college.columbia.edu/core/lithum
   /about.
4. "Art Humanities," Columbia College, accessed June 14, 2018,
   https://arthum.college.columbia.edu/.
5. "Music Humanities," Columbia College, accessed June 14, 2018,
   https://www.college.columbia.edu/core/classes/mh.php.
6. "Welcome," Frontiers of Science website, Columbia College,
   accessed June 14, 2018, http://ccnmtl.columbia.edu/projects
   /frontiers/.
7. "Frontiers of Science," Columbia College, accessed June 14, 2018,
   https://www.college.columbia.edu/core/classes/fos.php.

14. Departments

1. Neil Levy, "Downshifting and Meaning in Life," *Ratio* 18, no. 2
   (2005): 187–188.

17. A Tenure Case

1. The source is Paul J. Olscamp, *Moral Leadership: Ethics and the
   College Presidency* (Lanham, Md.: Rowman and Littlefield,

2003), 43–47. The material has been edited for the sake of continuity.

18. Autonomy

1. Professor X, *This Beats Working for a Living: The Dark Secrets of a College Professor* (New Rochelle, N.Y.: Arlington House, 1973), 11.

Index

academia, professors' view, 1–4
academic conferences, participation in, 1–2
academic freedom and tenure, 81–84
acronyms, 25–26
"Address to the Legislature of New York" (Stanton), 66
administration, 38–41, 75; choosing, 42–45; faculty view of, 2–3, 44–45, 79; quasi-administrative positions, 7–8, 75; support to departments, 57; turnover, 45
advisory system, 48
Aeneid (Virgil), 67
Aeschylus, 67
"Ain't I a Woman?" (Truth), 66
Al-Ghazali, 65
Amiens Cathedral, 69
American Philosophical Association, Eastern Division Meeting, 18
Anna Karenina, 73
anthropology, 59
appointment. *See* faculty
Aquinas, Thomas, 65
Aristotle, 65
Armstrong, Louis, 70
art: appreciation of, 53; exposure to, 61; history, 59, 62; requirement, 69–71; studio, 59; Western, 65

astronomy, 59
astrophysics, 71
Augustine, 65, 67
Austen, Jane, 68

Bacchae (Euripides), 67
Bach, Johann Sebastian, 70
Barzun, Jacques, 90
Beethoven, Ludwig van, 70
Bell, Daniel, 90
Berg, Alban, 70
Berlioz, Hector, 70
Bernini, Gian Lorenzo, 69
Bible, 65, 67
biodiversity, 71
biology, 59
Bither, Philip, 22–24
Boccaccio, 67
Bowling Green University, 85
Brandenburg Concertos, the (Bach), 70
Brann, Eva T. H., 50
Brown University, 11, 46, 48
Bruegel, Pieter, 69
Burke, Edmund, 66

Cage, John, 70
Cahn, Victor L., 19–24
celebrity faculty, 39–40

Cervantes, Miguel de, 68
chemistry, 59
Chopin, Frédéric, 70
Churchill, Winston, 83
City of God (Augustine), 65
City University of New York, 57; Graduate Center Philosophy Program, 29
clarity (pedagogic strategic step), 25–27, 28, 29–30; speaking too quickly, 25, 29–30; steps in reasoning, 26–27; using terminology, 25–26, 29–30
classics (language and the arts), 59
class size. *See* enrollment numbers
cognitive science, 59
Colby College, Summer School of Languages, 22, 23
Columbia University, 3; Columbia College, 64–72, 90; Department of Philosophy, 11
comparative literature, 59
computer science, 59
Confessions (Augustine), 67
Cooley, Rita, 61
Copland, Aaron, 70
course selection, 47
Crime and Punishment (Dostoevsky), 68
critical thinking, 53
curriculum areas, 59
curriculum committee, 56
curriculum requirements, 46–49, 55–58; core curriculum, 64–72; distribution requirements, 59–63, 64; mathematics, 55; science, 55; trading, 58

dance, 59
Dante, 67, 68
Darwin, Charles, 66
dean: office, 2, 45; role in faculty appointment/tenure, 76, 79, 80, 85–89; salary, 2; search, 42, 55. *See also* administration
Debussy, Achille-Claude, 70
Decameron (Boccaccio), 67
Democracy and Education (Dewey), 50
Democracy in America (Tocqueville), 66
democratic system of government, 52
departmental culture: changing, 33–37; discord, 73–75, 79–80, 84, 87; size, 76
departmental majors, requirements, 46
Descartes, René, 66
Dewey, John, 50
Die Feen (The Fairies), 7
Discipline and Punish (Foucault), 66
Discourse on Inequality (Rousseau), 66
"Doctor Fox" experiment, 8–9
Don Quixote (Cervantes), 68
Dostoevsky, Fyodor, 68
Du Bois, W.E.B., 66

Earth science, 71
economics, 59, 61, 63
Eisenhower, Dwight D., 3–4
Ellington, Duke, 70
English, 59: fundamentals, 62
enrollment numbers, 35, 40, 57–58, 60
Essays (Montaigne), 68
Ethics (Spinoza), 19
Euripides, 67
European civilization, 62
European culture, 62
evaluations, teaching, 30–32, 36, 85
examination/test, 29, 36
expository writing, 64

faculty: academic reputation, 2; appearing knowledgeable, 8–9; appointment, 73, 76–80; autonomy, 90–93; celebrity, 39–40; commitment to discipline, 2; demotion, 81; impact on students, 11–15, 27–28, 47, 72; insularity, 91–93; lateral transfer, 81; move to administration, 3; professional advancement, 1; promotion, 81, 85–89; recruiting outstanding teacher, 39; search, 76–80; specialization (*see* research pursuits); view of academia, 1–4; view of administration, 2–3, 45, 79; view of administrative search process, 45. *See also* faculty adviser; faculty hiring process; faculty salary; promotion; tenure

faculty adviser, 48

faculty hiring process: campus interview, 34; candidate's teaching approach, 34; interview questions, 34; position description, 33; recruiting researcher, 40

faculty salary, 2

Fanon, Frantz, 66

Foucault, Michel, 66

Freud Reader, 66

Freud, Sigmund, 66

funding, attracting, 40, 86, 88

Gandhi, Mohandas K., 66

Gay, Peter, 90

government, comparative, 62–63

Goya y Lucientes, Francisco, 69

graduate school, 5–10

graduate student. *See* student

Gregorian chant, 69

Groundwork of the Metaphysics of Morals (Kant), 66

Gurland, Robert, 27–28

Hadas, Moses, 90

Hampshire, Stuart, 18–19

Handel, George Frideric, 70

Harvard University, 27

Haydn, Franz Joseph, 70

Herodotus, 67

Heroides (Ovid), 67

Highet, Gilbert, 90

Hildegard of Bingen, 69

Hillerbrand, Hans, 66

Histories, The (Herodotus), 67

history, 59, 61

History of the Peloponnesian War (Thucydides), 67

Hobbes, Thomas, 66

Hofstadter, Richard, 90

Homer, 67

Hook, Sidney, 61

Husserl, Edmund, 92

Ibn Tufayl, 65

Inferno (Dante), 67, 68

Ives, Charles, 70

Jewett, John G., 55–56

job training, 52

Josquin des Prez, 69

Kant, Immanuel, 66

Kasparov, Garry, 51

King Lear (Shakespeare), 68

Kline, Morris, 61

Kusch, Polykarp, 90

language, foreign, 53–54, 56, 59, 61, 62, 64

language and the arts (curriculum area), 59, 60, 61

Le Corbusier, 69

lecture, invitation to present, 2

Leviathan (Hobbes), 66

liberal education: core curriculum, 64–72; curricular structure,

liberal education (*continued*)
46–49; distribution requirements,
59–63; requirements, 55–58;
self-justifying, 40–54
linguistic sensitivity, 53–54
literature: appreciation of, 53, 61;
development, 67; Western
Europe, 62
load. *See* teaching
Locke, John, 66
logic, 53
Lyrics (Sappho), 67

Machiavelli, 65
madrigal, the, 69
maritime studies, 59
Marx, Karl, 66
Marx-Engels Reader, 66
mathematics, 53; curriculum area,
59; requirement, 55–56, 60, 63
Mercersberg Academy, 19
Messiah (Handel), 70
Michelangelo, 69
Mill, John Stuart, 66
Milton, John, 68
Monet, Claude, 69
Montaigne, Michel de, 68
Monteverdi, 69
Morrison, Toni, 68
Morse, Sally, 86–89
motivation (pedagogic strategic
step), 17–21, 27, 28, 30; humor in
service of learning, 21, 28;
instructor's personality, 21–24, 28;
style of presentation, 21
Mozart, Wolfgang Amadeus, 70
music: appreciation of, 53; exposure
to, 61; history, 62; language and
the arts, 59; requirement, 69–71;
Western, 65

natural history, knowledge of, 53
neuroscience, 59, 71

New York University, 1, 27, 61;
Unified Studies Division of
Washington Square College of
Liberal Arts and Sciences, 62–63
"niche" department/discipline,
85–89
Nicomachean Ethics and Politics
(Aristotle), 65
Nietzsche, Friedrich Wilhelm, 66

Odyssey (Homer), 67
office hours, 13–14, 40, 91
Olscamp, Paul J., 85–89
O'Neill, Tip (Thomas P.), 73
On Liberty (Mill), 66
On the Genealogy of Morals
(Nietzsche), 66
Oresteia (Aeschylus), 67
organization (pedagogic strategic
step), 24–25, 27, 28, 30; planning,
25, 28, 66
Origin of Species and Descent of Man
(Darwin), 66
Ovid, 67

Paradise Lost (Milton), 68
Parker, Charlie, 70
Parthenon, 69
pedagogy: fundamentals of success,
17; mastering skills, 17, 28, 39;
principles of good, 9, 29. *See also*
teaching
philosophy, 54, 59, 60, 61, 65:
analysis, 62; development, 67
physical science, knowledge of, 53
physics, 59, 63
Picasso, Pablo, 69
Plato, 65, 67
policies and procedures manual,
87, 89
policy, institutional, 3
political science, 59, 61
Pollock, Jackson, 69

president (university), 3. *See also* administration
Pride and Prejudice (Austen), 68
Prince, The (Machiavelli), 65
Princeton University, 18–19
professor. *See* faculty
Professor X, 90
promotion, 35–36
Protestant Reformation, 66
provost: office, 2; salary, 2; search committee, 42. *See also* administration
psychology, 59, 62
publishing efforts: assistance, 35; authoring/editing books, 1; professional/refereed journals, 1, 5, 85–87

Quine, Willard Van Orman, 27
Qur'an, 65

Rabi, I. I., 4
Raphael, 69
Reflections on the Revolution in France (Burke), 66
religion, 59
Rembrandt van Rijn, 69
Republic (Plato), 65
requirements. *See* curriculum requirements
research pursuits: as opportunity, 2; priority, 1, 35, 74, 85–88, 90; recruiting, 40; release time from teaching, 6–8, 38; specialization, 5, 6–7, 38, 57, 60, 68, 74–75, 79, 93
Rite of Spring, The (Stravinsky), 70
Rousseau, Jean-Jacques, 66

salary. *See* faculty salary; *specific administrative title*
Sappho, 67
Schapiro, Meyer, 90
Schonberg, Arnold, 70

Schubert, Franz Peter, 70
science: curriculum area, 59; exposure to, 61; laboratory, 56, 63; requirement, 55–56, 60, 63, 64, 65
scientific method, 53
scientific revolution, 66
Second Treatise (Locke), 66
Sellars, Wilfrid, 18, 19
Sepulveda, 66
service to university, 1, 74, 85, 88, 90, 91, 93
Shakespeare, William, 68
Shamos, Morris, 61
Skidmore College, 19
Smith, Adam, 66
Social Contract (Rousseau), 66
social science, knowledge of, 53, 62
social studies (curriculum area), 59, 60
sociology, 59, 61, 62
Song of Solomon (Morrison), 68
Souls of Black Folk, The (Du Bois), 66
"Souls of White Folk" (Du Bois), 66
speaker presentation, 82–83
Spinoza, Baruch, 19
St. John's College, 50
staff (university), 3. *See also* administration
Stanton, Elizabeth Cady, 66
statistics, 59
Stravinsky, Igor, 70
student: advising, 2; beneficiary of core curriculum, 71; concern to professor, 1, 2; enthusiasm for learning, 21; graduate student, 6, 29–32; involving in learning, 21; teacher's impact on, 11–15, 27–28, 39, 55; undergraduate student, 29. *See also* evaluations, teaching; graduate student; undergraduate student
The Subjection of Women (Mill and Taylor), 66

"Swaraj" (On self-rule; Gandhi), 66
Swarthmore College, 22
syllabus, 29, 36
Symphonie fantastique (Berlioz), 70
Symposium (Plato), 67

Taurasi, Diana, 51
Taylor, Harriet, 66
Taylor, Richard, 11–15, 16
teaching: across disciplines, 71;
    autonomy, 90–93; avoiding, 7;
    class enrollment, 40; duties, 6;
    ease of, 5–10; ethical obligations,
    29, 47, 55; graduate students to
    teach, 29–32; importance of
    excellence, 33, 38; levels of
    effectiveness, 39; load, 2;
    methodology, 74–75; observing
    faculty, 35; personality, 21–22;
    practicing, 29; priority of, 1, 2, 33,
    35, 74; prizes, 38; release from,
    6–8, 38; self-assessment of skills,
    40–41; strategic steps, 17, 27 (*see
    also* clarity; motivation;
    organization); success, 16–17, 27,
    47, 87, 88, 89, 90–91, 93;
    team-taught course, 7. *See also*
    curriculum requirements;
    pedagogy
tenure: academic freedom and,
    81–84, 91–92; awarding, 36–37;
    case described, 85–89; decisions,
    35–36, 83–84; mechanics of
    system, 81–82; revoked, 81
test. *See* examination
theater, 59
*This Beats Working for a Living: The
    Dark Secrets of a College Professor*
    (Professor X), 90
Thucydides, 67
Tocqueville, Alexis de, 66
To the Lighthouse (Woolf), 68
Treatise on Moral Sentiments
    (Smith), 66
Trilling, Lionel, 90
Truth, Sojourner, 66

undergraduate student. *See* student
University of Pittsburgh, 18
University of Vermont, 23:
    Department of Philosophy,
    34, 55

Verdi, Giuseppe, 70
Vindication of the Rights of Woman, A
    (Wollstonecraft), 66
Virgil, 67
Vitoria, Francisco de, 66
vocational education, 52

Wagner, Richard, 70
Warhol, Andy, 69
Wealth of Nations (Smith), 66
Western civilization (requirement),
    56, 65
Western Europe, literature of,
    62, 65
Western Washington University, 85
West Point Academy (United States
    Military Academy), 28
Williams College, 59
Wollstonecraft, Mary, 66
Woolf, Virginia, 68
world history, knowledge of, 53
Wozzeck (Berg), 70
Wright, Frank Lloyd, 69
The Wretched of the Earth (Fanon), 66
writing, expository, 64

About the Author

STEVEN M. CAHN is professor emeritus of philosophy at the City University of New York Graduate Center, where he served for nearly a decade as provost and vice president for academic affairs, then as acting president.

He was born in Springfield, Massachusetts, in 1942. His early years were devoted to the piano, which he studied with Herbert Stessin of the Juilliard School and the renowned chamber music artist Artur Balsam. After earning an AB from Columbia College in 1963 and PhD in philosophy from Columbia University in 1966, Dr. Cahn taught at Dartmouth College, Vassar College, New York University, the University of Rochester, and the University of Vermont, where he chaired the Department of Philosophy.

He then served as a program officer at the Exxon Education Foundation, as acting director for humanities at the Rockefeller Foundation, and as the first director of general programs at the National Endowment for the Humanities. He formerly chaired the American Philosophical Association's Committee on the Teaching of Philosophy, was the association's delegate to the American Council of Learned Societies, and was longtime president of the John Dewey Foundation.

Dr. Cahn is the author of fourteen books, including *Fate, Logic, and Time*; *Saints and Scamps: Ethics in Academia,*

25th anniversary edition; *From Student to Scholar: A Candid Guide to Becoming a Professor*; *Polishing Your Prose* (with Victor L. Cahn); *Happiness and Goodness: Philosophical Reflections on the Good Life* (with Christine Vitrano); and *Religion Within Reason*.

He has edited or coedited nearly fifty books, many in multiple editions, including *Moral Problems in Higher Education*; *The World of Philosophy*, now in its second edition; *Exploring Philosophy of Religion*, now in its second edition; *Classic and Contemporary Readings in the Philosophy of Education*, now in its second edition; *The Affirmative Action Debate*, now in its second edition; *Political Philosophy*, now in its third edition; *Exploring Ethics*, now in its fourth edition; *Exploring Philosophy*, now in its sixth edition; and *Classics of Western Philosophy*, now in its eighth edition.

Dr. Cahn has also served as general editor of four multivolume series: *Blackwell Philosophy Guides*; *Blackwell Readings in Philosophy*; *Issues in Academic Ethics*; and *Critical Essays on the Classics*.

His numerous articles have appeared in a broad spectrum of publications, including the *Journal of Philosophy*, the *Chronicle of Higher Education*, *Shakespeare Quarterly*, the *American Journal of Medicine*, the *New Republic*, and the *New York Times*.

A collection of essays written in his honor, edited by two of his former doctoral students, Robert B. Talisse of Vanderbilt University and Maureen Eckert of the University of Massachusetts Dartmouth, is titled *A Teacher's Life: Essays for Steven M. Cahn*.

Printed in the United States
By Bookmasters